Just Good Politics

Just Good Politics

The Life of Raymond Chafin, Appalachian Boss

■

RAYMOND CHAFIN
and
TOPPER SHERWOOD

UNIVERSITY OF PITTSBURGH PRESS
Pittsburgh and London

Published by the University of Pittsburgh Press, Pittsburgh, Pa. 15260
Copyright © 1994, Raymond Chafin and Topper Sherwood
All rights reserved
Manufactured in the United States of America
Printed on acid-free paper
Second printing, 1996

Library of Congress Cataloging-in-Publication Data
Chafin, Raymond, 1917–
    Just good politics : the life of Raymond Chafin, Appalachian boss
  / Raymond Chafin and Topper Sherwood.
      p.   cm.
    Includes index.
    ISBN 0-8229-3789-1 (cl)
    1. Chafin, Raymond, 1917–   2. West Virginia—Politics
and government. 3. Politicians—West Virginia—Biography.
I. Sherwood, Topper.   II. Title.
F245.42.C47A3   1994
975.4'043'092—dc20
[B]   93-44810
                                                                                                      CIP

A CIP catalogue record for this book is available from the British Library.
Eurospan, London

    We wish to acknowledge the assistance of people at various agencies, including the Kanawha County Public Library, the West Virginia State Archives, West Virginia Secretary of State Ken Hechler, June Payne and Jim Cedrone at the John Fitzgerald Kennedy Library, and former West Virginia Welfare Commissioner W. Bernard Smith.
    Wayne M. Davis, of the Associated Press, graciously offered edition comments while working as a visiting professor at Marshall University.
    Most of all, we wish to thank our families—especially Louise Chambers Chafin for her additions and Margaret Chafin Williams for her persistence—as well as "transplanted" Logan Countian David B. Holland, who brought us all together.

■ "Kennedy's supreme political cleverness was to temporarily, but totally and sincerely, renounce politics and to transform himself internally for others and for himself into a man of exigency.... The West Virginian did not choose the political Kennedy, about whom he knew nothing, but the one whom he had seen with his own eyes.... In short, West Virginians required that the future president put ethical action in the place of politics."

—Jean-Paul Sartre,
"Kennedy and West Virginia," *Morality and History*

■ "Anything from $2 to $5 buys a vote [in Logan County] on election day, and sometimes they are delivered in wholesale lots. Moonshine is still used as payment for a vote, but it is now risky business.... There is every likelihood that if they [Kennedy and Humphrey] did buy votes, they would be double-crossed on election day."

—From an article in *Life* magazine, May 9, 1960

■ "In West Virginia, everything's political except politics. And that's personal."

—West Virginia saying

Contents

	Preface	ix
	Introduction	3
1	Cow Creek	6
2	Appalachian Spring	18
3	Work and Politics	32
4	1936: First Election	45
5	Big Bad John	60
6	Politics	75
7	Inroads	89
8	Ray Watts and Fiddlin' Bob Byrd	105
9	Kennedy	115
10	The 1960 Election	130
11	White House Emissary	151
12	1964–1984: Moore and Rockefeller	159
13	1988: One More Time	175
	Epilogue: Politics Old and New	188
	Index	193

Preface

I hesitated when Raymond Chafin first approached me with the idea of writing his autobiography. At least one local newspaper routinely identified him as a "Logan County political boss," which constituted not one, but two strikes against him. People like me, in the more urban parts of West Virginia, often look down their noses at Logan County, much in the same way that cosmopolitan America often appraises West Virginia itself. Logan, along with the other southern coal counties—Mingo, McDowell, Wyoming, Boone, and Mercer—has long been shrouded by a dark history, known as one of those mountainous territories where coal miners scrape out dirty and difficult lives, where people live in hillside cabins, and where "politics" means "kin." Most stories about Logan carried in Charleston newspapers are negative; they deal with poverty, violence, mining accidents, and, not least, political corruption. These are the images that first came to mind when I anticipated having dinner with Logan County's leading "political boss." By the same token, these stories—combined with my own label, "Charleston journalist"—likely did little to inspire Chafin's confidence in me.

From that first meeting, Raymond Chafin surprised me by not conforming to my idea of the stereotypical Appalachian politician. I had expected a white-collar political broker/financier, adept at all the tricks and chicanery that journalists often wonder about but rarely describe in print. Instead I was introduced to a congenial man whose faded blue shirt had tiny cigarette burns in it. Chafin didn't give the impression of someone who'd made a lot of money in his life—from politics or anything else—and he answered all my questions with disarming candor. He struck me less like a political power broker than a bricklayer come straight from the job site.

Indeed, as I came to know him better, I learned that construction work had actually been Raymond Chafin's primary source of income during his entire political career. Although power can itself be a bargaining chip, he wielded at least as much political clout by being able to produce roads, bridges, dams, and schools for Logan County. He has also built a constituency of voters who have supported, more often than not, "his" candidates over a generation of election days. In a backhanded defense of machine politics, Theodore Roosevelt once said that the successful political boss "is very apt to be a man who, in addition to committing wickedness in his own interest, also does look after the interests of others," and that any boss who acts only for himself "would probably last but a short time in any community." The people who greet Raymond Chafin on the street every day seem, in any case, to be satisfied with his work. "I never wanted much for myself," he says with a wink. "I just liked to win 'em."

During my first conversations with Chafin, I was eager—as most readers will be—to hear about the historic West Virginia primary campaign of 1960. It was, after all, John F. Kennedy's hard-won victory there that caused his strongest Democratic rival, Hubert H. Humphrey, to withdraw from the race, clinching Kennedy's nomination for president. Ever since the last vote was tallied that spring, analysts have speculated about the effects of vote buying and "out-of-state wealth" on JFK's victory. Investigations were carried out by the U.S. Justice Department, the FBI, anti-Kennedy Democrats, the *Wall Street Journal,* local newspapers, and Washington exposeur Jack Anderson. Invariably the conclusion was, as one former state governor declared (intending no apparent irony), that Kennedy had "sold himself" to the voters, not bought them.[1]

Still, the issue will not die. In a *New York Times* article in 1992, West Virginia novelist Denise Giardina wrote that the Kennedy campaign "overwhelmed Hubert Humphrey in West Virginia by putting large sums of money in the pockets of local officials." Her *Unquiet Earth,* in fact, fictionalizes Chafin's own legendary misunderstanding with Kennedy financiers, a story told in these pages.[2] But *Just Good Politics* doesn't merely satisfy one's curiosity about the 1960 campaign. Just as fulfilling is Chafin's description of a political culture that has endured in southern West Virginia for some time. Certainly many politicians have tried to tell their stories; others have had their stories told through prosecutors and grand juries. None, however, can offer with Chafin's color or candor the behind-the-scenes deals, the polling-place maneuverings, and, perhaps most importantly, the political influence of larger bureaucratic interests on elections in this region.

Readers will quickly discern that Raymond Chafin describes a world that is not in line with the shining democratic principles they learned in school or those offered by the ponderous pundits trotted onto the screen each election day. Chafin describes deal making, rigged elections, and votes bought with cash and

1. Dan B. Fleming, Jr., *Kennedy vs. Humphrey, 1960: The Pivotal Battle for the Democratic Presidential Nomination* (Jefferson, N.C.: McFarland & Company, Inc., 1992), p. 145.

2. *New York Times,* 31 October 1992, sec. 1, p. 21, col. 2; Denise Giardina, *Unquiet Earth* (New York: W. W. Norton, 1992). Also of interest are Giardina's *Good King Harry* (New York: Harper & Row, 1984) and *Storming Heaven* (New York: W. W. Norton, 1987).

whiskey. He tells us about men who were shot for siding with the wrong people in the wrong district during the wrong election. For all his cynical realism, however, we can trace most of the political practices described in this book to institutions likely to have been familiar to our country's early voters.

Identifiable elements in the political culture of southern West Virginia, in fact, date back to the days before the American Revolution, to the British Colony of Virginia. The high-born gentlemen of the Old Dominion were trading votes for pints long before any "moonshiners" appeared in Appalachia. Magisterial representatives were routinely chosen by the most wealthy landowners. Candidates were still forced, however, to compete for support, and many a gentleman won his laurels only after defying election laws and treating his voting neighbors to a drink. George Washington and another candidate reportedly gave Alexandria's populace "a Hogshead of Toddy" on election day in 1774.[3]

Aristocratic Virginians later developed what historian John Alexander Williams calls a tradition of "oral political culture," defined as politicians "traveling from place to place, making speeches and developing supporters on a face-to-face, friends-and-neighbors basis."[4] Successful candidates attracted followers with personal friendship and favors. Like some formal Virginia institutions, the oral tradition persisted in West Virginia—especially in the southern counties—long after the new state was established in 1863. Political patronage, similarly, remains familiar to most modern-day voters in both Virginias and elsewhere.

Virginia's nineteenth-century political institutions also included a "court day," the day on which the circuit judge came to

3. Edward N. Saveth, *Understanding the American Past* (Boston, Mass.: Little Brown & Co., 1954), p. 91.
4. John Alexander Williams, *West Virginia: A History for Beginners* (Charleston, W. Va.: Appalachian Editions, 1993), p. 111.

a particular county to hold trials. Court day, occurring several times a year, became as much a social institution as a political one, according to Williams:

> Many people watched the trials as a form of entertainment, but others came to visit, gossip or shop. The county militia . . . usually held its drills on court day; young men competed in foot races and other athletics. There were shooting matches. . . . It was an occasion for people to visit their friends and relatives from other parts of the county. (Williams, p. 109)

What was true for court day became true for election day, which historian Altina Waller calls "the most important social event of the year." In the late nineteenth century, election-day politicians faced off against supporters and hecklers alike, and voters cast their votes aloud, publicly: "Everyone in the community was fully aware, not only of everyone else's political beliefs, but of their status as landowners or tenants and their family connections. Men came to the elections prepared to state and defend their politics as well as their reputations, if necessary."[5] Such an environment insured not only that people and politicians met, literally, on common ground, but that elections retained a free-for-all, hand-to-hand quality—not the media events they have become in most parts of the country today.

Raymond Chafin describes Logan County elections in much the same terms. He remembers when political candidates "came out to where you lived. They found you in your cornfield and told you what they stood for." His family and friends "stuck together [and] voted together. And that," he says, "made them

---

5. Altina Waller, *Feud: Hatfields, McCoys, and Social Change in Appalachia, 1860–1900* (Chapel Hill, N.C.: University of North Carolina Press, 1988), p. 16.

powerful." Chafin's "Pony Express" meetings (described in chapter 6), the role of political patronage, and the use of slates all date back to a time when politics demanded more from voters—and perhaps offered more—than present-day iterative polling and tabulation. The political terminology is the same, but the impersonalized electronic networks that dominate the electoral process today are far removed from the political traditions of court day.

Face-to-face politics, on the other hand, can also be as far removed from the democratic ideal as they are from the media marketeering of today. Waller reminds us that many of the "clan feud" battles occurred at the polling place; Chafin tells how "dangerous" local politics could be, and he recounts the election-day murder of his own father-in-law. "If you didn't go out there and risk getting shot or killed," he reminds us, "you didn't work an election at all."

One can only imagine the musings of John F. Kennedy as he entered West Virginia's active political culture. We cannot know, of course, what Kennedy thought as he approached the 1960 primary. We do know that he had been reading up on West Virginia history and that he continued to be interested in the subject during the campaign. That April, Kennedy was scanning a map of the Mountain State while flying to Charleston on his private plane—shortly before meeting Chafin for the first time. (It is ironic that the leader of the first national media campaign would soon find himself immersed in the old-fashioned politics of Raymond Chafin.) Kennedy interrogated his companion, U.S. Congressman Ken Hechler, with questions about the state's history.

"Tell me about . . . the Indians," Kennedy asked Hechler, letting his finger wander through Mingo and Logan counties.

The West Virginia congressman offered what he could, but was amazed to realize that the Massachusetts senator knew more than he did about West Virginia's bloody frontier war.

PREFACE

"The Iroquois Confederacy produced great characters," Kennedy commented. He ticked off the names of several Indian leaders, including Logan, an eloquent Mingo speaker who negotiated treaties for the Iroquois. Logan's entire family was killed by white settlers in April 1774. Kennedy gazed out the airplane window and quoted the leader's most famous speech, condemning the men who betrayed his trust: "Who is left to mourn for Logan? Not one."

There are indeed few left to mourn for today's Logan, a county condemned as "backward" by generations of urban journalists. Raymond Chafin tells something of Logan's story in these pages. Some will read it as a series of funny or clever anecdotes—"Br'er Rabbit" tales told by a wizened mountaineer from the strip-mined hillside that was once his grandparent's homestead. *Just Good Politics,* however, offers more than that. It is a genuine bridge between our increasingly homogenized American society and a largely unexamined part of rural mountain life. Like so many other cultures, West Virginia's traditional political culture may have something to teach us, even as it disappears with progress and the passage of time.

Topper Sherwood
Charleston, West Virginia
1993

Just Good Politics

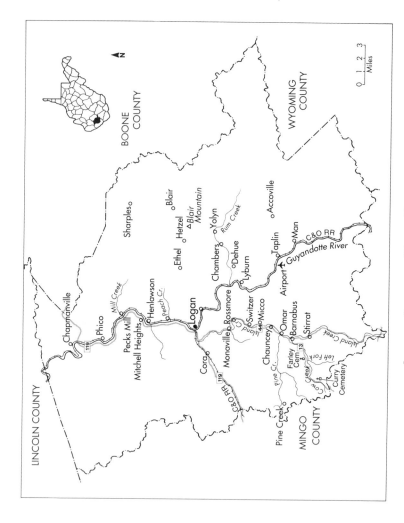

Logan County, West Virginia

Introduction

RAIN PATTERED AGAINST THE ROOF OF THE yellow cab as it pulled up to the White House gate. The door opened and a stocky, bald man in his mid-forties climbed out, offering his pass to a guard. The visitor waited nervously while the guard made a phone call, and soon someone came out with an umbrella. The visitor walked with his escort through the rain, up the curving driveway and into the west wing of the presidential mansion.

Inside, the visitor was asked again to show his pass, along with some other identification. He produced a West Virginia driver's license and gazed around, awed by the lavish furnishings. His identity confirmed, the man was shown to a reception room where he was told to wait. He took a seat.

To some of the White House staff who saw him sitting there that day, Raymond Chafin must have looked more than a little awkward. Busy young political aides, clad in Brooks Brothers, bustled past as he nervously adjusted his bow tie and checked the cut of his brand-new blue herringbone suit.

Certainly the rest of the country was concerned with other matters than the one that brought Raymond Chafin to the White House that day. Soviet Cosmonaut Yuri Gagarin was preparing to become the first human in space. Martin Luther King, Jr., now in his early thirties, was rising from relative obscurity to "a position of power and prominence in the struggle against racial codes and customs," according to the *New York Times*. Southeast Asians were firing the first shots of what would become the hottest battle of the Cold War, and world leaders were wondering how the new U.S. president would deal with his volatile Soviet counterpart when they met later that spring. But before he faced off with Khrushchev, John F. Kennedy was working to put his own house in order, tackling a long list of domestic issues. One of these issues was especially important to him, as it was to Raymond Chafin—hence his visit to the White House on this rainy day in the winter of 1961.

As he waited, this son of a West Virginia timber hauler was literally shaking in his new shoes. After all, through these halls had passed presidents and dignitaries stretching back to the time of John Adams. Raymond's thoughts turned to Mary Chafin Curry, his grandmother, who peddled homemade goods on horseback. He thought about his Uncle Harley of Cow Creek and the other family members and friends who had helped him become the chief political power broker in his own obscure part of the world. With thoughts of these people—*his* people—Raymond Chafin calmed himself as he waited to see the president of the United States.

John F. Kennedy was not unfamiliar with Raymond's world. Indeed, it was a place he'd visited only the year before, and he never forgot the experience. How could anyone forget the muddy, unpaved roads made almost unnavigable by common rain; coal miners who'd been stricken with "miner's asthma"—black lung; or bare-footed children dining on little more than government-surplus bread and lard? More than anything else he'd seen during his 1960 campaign, the scenes of Appalachian poverty had touched John Kennedy's heart.

His waiting finally done, Raymond was told that the president was ready. Rising, he was shown into the executive office, the famous Oval Room looking out on the Rose Garden and the Washington Monument beyond. At one end of the room, two comfortable sofas flanked a small coffee table next to a marble fireplace. On the other, a row of French doors and windows illuminated the president's desk, a huge oak piece hand-carved from the timbers of a nineteenth-century British sailing vessel. Kennedy's favored wicker rocking chair sat out in front.

Kennedy came around the desk and greeted his visitor warmly. He offered Raymond a chair and pulled his rocker up close. Both men were getting settled when a secretary came in with a schedule and a pronouncement: Mr. Chafin had ten minutes to conclude his business with the president. Kennedy looked up.

"I called this man in here to see me," he corrected. "He has all the time he needs."

1 Cow Creek

BARNABUS CURRY AND HIS FAMILY WERE the first people I know of who settled along Cow Creek in Logan County. They came here sometime in the last century. Barnabus was my mother's grandpa. The town of Barnabus was named after him. He owned all this land, all the acreage up and down the creek and all the bottomlands too. He was married three or four times and had about twenty children. He was a farmer, just like all of them up here back then.

The houses you see along the creek today used to be cornfields. The land was steep, but they farmed it. They raised beets, corn, potatoes, and beans—just about everything you have today. No eggplant, though. Nobody knew what eggplant was back then.

Here, at the head of the creek, there were only three houses. There was Pleasant Curry—we called him "Plez"—he had himself a family; and my Great Uncle Victor Curry—he had him a family; and Victor's brother, Tommy, who was married to Mary Chafin Curry. They were my grandparents, and they just about raised me.

COW CREEK

You ought to picture how people lived when my grandpa and grandma moved into the head of this creek. The Currys owned everything up here and they divided it together. Barnabus gave Grandpa Tommy the head of the creek and Victor got all the land further down. The upper end, following the creek southwest, belonged to the Brownings. They played it smart, marrying into the Currys, and they really had the farm tools: hayrakes and mowing machines, all horse-drawn.

Back before 1900, Grandpa Tommy Curry moved from the head of the creek and built himself a house at the foot of Cow Creek Mountain. It was a big house of chestnut timber with a wraparound porch on it. Tommy was an ox-driver. (Oxen aren't like horses; they all pull at once. You put eight or ten of them together and you have yourself a steady-pulling thing.) The coal mines were starting in about then, and Tommy figured if he moved down to the bottom of the hill he could make himself a little money helping people pull their buggies up that mountain on their way to Williamson. It might be gardeners, a doctor, or a lawyer—anyone with just one horse. When they got to the bottom of that hill, they hollered for Grandpa Tommy, and he came out with his team. He hooked it up to that buggy or wagon and made a four-mule out of it. They gave him a quarter or fifty cents for pulling that thing to the top of the hill for them.

My father's father, Thomas Chafin, did the same thing for people on the other side of the mountain, the Mingo County side. It was steeper over there, and he used his pack mules to carry people's things up the hill. Thomas Chafin spent his early days as a carpenter. He farmed and was a preacher too. His sister, my Great Aunt Levicy, married Devil Anse Hatfield.[1]

---

1. "Devil" Anse Hatfield was leader of the Hatfield clan in the famed Hatfield-McCoy feud along the West Virginia-Kentucky border from 1860 to 1900.—T. S.

My grandfather's first wife was one of Barnabus Curry's daughters, and they had three children before she died. Then he married a Browning and they had four more, including Elbert, my daddy. The parents divorced when their kids were young, and most of them went to live with other relatives. My daddy was mostly raised by Victor and Betty Curry, and he married Lucinda Curry, which brought me closer to the Currys than anybody else.

My other grandpa's name was Thomas, too, but everybody called him Tommy—Tommy Curry. He was the finest old man you ever seen, my granddaddy was. Kind of easygoing, but he was a hard, hard-working man. He worked every day, mostly saw-logging and pulling timber out of these hills. Of a summertime, he'd go and work his farm. Or the coal operators would come and get him to haul timbers and ceiling props way down the creek to the mines. Tommy got fifty or seventy-five cents a day to go off on a timber drive. He'd be gone through the week and come home on weekends; then he stayed busy there too. There was always something for him to do.

Grandpa Tommy had his brother, Victor Curry, do all his dealing for him. Victor was better educated for one thing, and Tommy had bad feet. Victor did all the trading for a lot of people up here. He wasn't a merchant, but he'd come to buy and sell stuff for them. He drove his big, two-ton wagon out of the hollow to the city of Logan. When he came back, he had a barrel or two of flour or something for my people.

Victor was a good-sized man with a handlebar moustache. He was a smart old fellow, what we called "shifty"—working all the time, moving all the time, always with something to do. Victor might be talking to you, but you knew he was always thinking of how to make another dollar around the hill someplace. I called Uncle Victor "Grandpa" too, because he helped raise my daddy.

Victor and Betty's place was a big, two-story house with a real nice garden. Aunt Betts was a Chafin and that made her sassy. She was the boss of all of them, including Victor and my grandpa. She didn't care what she said. I know one of my uncles built the house where I was born of hewed-out chestnut and poplar logs, right up here at the head of the creek. It was about twenty-four foot long and about fourteen foot wide, one window, and roofed with boards—just like we use shingles now. That house didn't have a nail in it. The logs were notched so they fit just as tight as they could be. Then the cracks were daubed, inside and out, with clay from the creek—and that clay would get just as hard as cement.

You'd be surprised how warm that house was. You could sleep anywhere in it, just put yourself a bed down—just something under you—and go to sleep. They weren't digging much coal yet in those days, so they fired it with wood. There were two rooms, each about twelve by fourteen foot, divided by a partition they put in there. We called it a house back then. I suppose they'd call it a "shanty" now.

They usually kept the kitchen a little better than any other room. It had an oak floor. The fireplace was two or three foot deep, and they could put several good-sized logs in. They hung big, black kettles from a piece of iron in the fireplace and cooked hominy and other stuff all day long. You could smell it cooking all day. It smelled real good.

There was a big snow on the night I was born—January 29, 1917. It was cold enough to freeze the creek and they had no way of getting a doctor up there, so "Aunt" Sally Curry acted as a midwife for all the women around. She lived about a mile down the creek. That night, my dad went down to get his grandma to stay with my mother. Then he had to go further on down, through the snow, after Aunt Sally. They got back here about the time I was born. Then Sally moved in with us to take care of my momma and me. I don't know how they did it—kind of how the squirrels take care of theirs, I guess. And here I am, seventy-seven years old today. We moved out of that house when I was just a kid, and it sat there for years after we moved out. There's a strip mine over there now.

Eventually, there were eight of us at home. Besides me, there was Bessie, Ester-May, Willie, Verna, Junior, Kenneth, and Clifton. I'm the oldest but, by God, every one of us was raised the hard way. For example, people did their own doctoring in those days. If a horse cut itself on a piece of barbed wire, we just put turpentine on it to keep the flies off. If a youngster cut his foot real bad, one of the older folks held him down, took a needle and white thread, and sewed it up. You just put your hand over your mouth and screamed, by God.

We saved our fruit jars for canning because we didn't have a whole lot of them to spare. Anytime somebody took apples or beans from a jar, that jar was saved. Around the garden, we had fence palings—wooden rails, rived from chestnut. They sloped those palings sharp on top so the chickens wouldn't fly up there, and they washed those fruit jars and hung them on those palings.

The Currys had maybe twenty-five or thirty head of cattle all together, and, in the spring of the year, they "ranged them back"—turned them loose in the woods. You could walk around in the hills anywhere you wanted to back then because those cattle kept it all cleaned out. Of a weekend, somebody went out and hunted up those cattle. They might be over at the head of this holler or way down yonder, another mile or so. One or two of those bulls might have a bell on. Nobody had nose rings, so they marked the cattle's ears—split the left, or cropped the right. That mark meant the animal belonged to Tommy Curry, or Plez Curry, or to one of the Dutys on the other side of the hill. Everybody had a piece of paper hanging on their kitchen wall telling them whose mark was whose, and they reported to each other where their cattle were.

"Hey, we saw your cows down by Liar Lick yesterday," a visitor would say. Or, "Your steer was at our place this morning! He's doing all right. Come get him anytime you want."

Then, in the fall, someone would come to Victor's place and say, "Hey, Aunt Betty! When were you planning on killing that beef?"

"Well, I don't know," Betty might say. "You want us to kill one?"

"Yeah. You go ahead and kill yours and bring us down a quarter; and when we kill ours, we'll bring you back a quarter."

So they decided to kill a beef that way, and everybody came to help with the job. They hung it up, butchered it, and, if the weather got warm, they cooked and canned some of it. I was a pretty good-sized boy by that time, so they sent me out to that paling fence.

"Raymond, get out there and get them cans in here," they said. "Now, you be careful, boy! Don't you break 'em!"

I went out and the palings were so high I needed a box to stand on. I let my little sister Bessie carry one. I wouldn't let her carry two; she was too small for that.

So they cut the meat, cooked it up, and put it in those jars. They sealed it, turning them upside down so the grease would come to the top and seal it double. Then those jars went into the cellar, and when we wanted steak we just brought up a can for dinner.

We had pork too. There was maybe a hundred head of hogs running around in this country then. In the fall they fed on chestnuts and acorns, which we called "mast."

"We're having good mast this year," the old folks said. "It'll be a good year for our hogs."

There was wild boar, too, but the young boys tried to shoot every boar they could find in those woods. The boar could kill your hunting dogs, and they ate them too! Also, you didn't want the boars mixing with your hogs. They multiply fast and, once they start in a country, wild boar is a hard thing to kill out. We cooked and ate wild boar whenever anybody brought one in.

We kids grew up with plenty of work to do, but there was play, too. It was around 1924 when I saw my first Victrola, the kind you crank up. My dad went to Logan and bought us one, the first of anybody on the creek. They all came around to look at that thing and listen. We kids could play it anytime we wanted, but my mother was the only one to crank it. She was afraid we'd break the spring. People took care of things in those days.

Of a summertime, we kids would do our swimming in a wide part of the creek. It was our swimming pool, usually about three- or four-foot deep, but sometimes we'd dam the creek with brush to make it even deeper. Then our parents came to tear it out. They thought we'd get drowned if it got too deep. We swam "skip-a-doo"—skinny-dippin'—back then too.

Drummers—salesmen—would come through every once in a while. A lot of times they asked for something to eat, and my family always said, "Sure, we'll fix you something!" They never did charge anything, but the drummers always left a dime or a nickel, like a tip. If it was a pack peddler, he stayed overnight and left them a dress or a shirt or something. It was a good life. We had plenty to eat; I didn't have to worry too much in those days.

Back in the early twenties, nobody had enough money to pay taxes for the roads. But nobody had a car, either. You couldn't hardly get a car up Cow Creek; it just wasn't that kind of road. The road went right up through the creek. In summertime, the doctor might get his T-model Ford up here, but that was it. Instead of paying road taxes, they had a fellow called an "overseer." The county paid the overseer maybe ten dollars a year to take care of the roads in his area. He gathered all the neighbors up; they came with their hoes and maddocks and maybe a mule and a plow. They went to where the creek had washed out a little bit, and they fixed it to where they could get the wagons through again. The men who owned horses took brush hooks and cut overhead so you wouldn't knock your hat off when you rode under the trees. That went on, I'd say, up until about 1930, after the mines had been working a while. They quit the overseer then because people got to paying taxes after that.

The first coal mines were put in at Pidgeon Creek, over on the Mingo County side of the mountain. The Chafins owned all the land around there—around Turner and Ragland—but they didn't know what it was worth. The coal speculators came in and those Chafins practically gave that land away. The companies had already started putting up houses for their workers and they talked about building schools. One fellow told the Chafins his company would name a school after them if they sold their land to him. That closed the deal. Yessir, that family must have really thought they were getting something when that company named a school after them.

By the early 1920s, the mines were really coming in. Most of the coal companies weren't from around here; they came in from Pittsburgh, New York, and places like that. I know there were at least twenty to twenty-five little mines along Island Creek, from Logan on up. There were big mines too, each working hundreds of men. More and more people moved in here then, and the companies built houses for just about all of them. You'd be surprised at the number of houses along Island Creek then. I'd say there were three or four thousand families—about ten times the number there now.

I don't remember the names of all those little companies but, eventually, Main Island Creek came in and bought them all out. Main Island Creek's people worked and tunneled and joined a whole bunch of those little mines underground. They ran long tracks around, inside and out, and brought all the coal to one big coal tipple, a separation plant, outside. Later, an even bigger company came along and bought out Main Island Creek.

Everywhere there was a little seam of coal, somebody came along and put in a mine. There must have been twenty-five coal companies from Logan to Stirrat—and each one of them had their own store. George Chambers was a man who came in to work for one of those company stores. He married another one of my aunts we called "Levicy." Her name was Louisa Curry. After three or four years, George and Louisa were separated. He left here and got into some kind of trouble. A bunch of federal people came in, hunting for him. We never did know what it was, but we didn't see George Chambers around here anymore after that.

Grandma Mary Curry, Grandpa Tommy's wife, did the peddling for our family. Of a summertime, she did most of the "goin' "—to town, that is—and she peddled things along the way. On a goin' day, Grandma Mary wore her riding skirt and black straw hat. She fixed that hat down with a long hat-pin stuck deep into the twist of hair on top of her head. They got me dressed up too. After getting scrubbed real good, I put on the best overalls I had. But no shoes; not in the summertime. You only got one pair of shoes each year, and you saved them as best you could.

By first daylight, Grandma Mary was out with the animals, getting everything ready. Her pack mule was loaded with beans, corn, and rhubarb (which we called "pie plant" then)—all food that we'd raised ourselves. Grandma tied it all down to the mule, and then she got up on her horse. She wasn't a real big woman, but she could get on that horse from just about anywhere—without climbing on the fence or anything. I'd climb up behind her and pull that old pack mule behind us as we rode, Grandma Mary talking to me the whole way along. "One day," she said,

"There's gonna be a big railroad up this creek. . . ." Or, "Winter's comin', Raymond! We've got to put up those beans when we get home. Ought to gather in our corn, too. . . ." *Our* corn, she said. Everything was "ours" to Grandma Mary. There wasn't nothing "hers." Everything was "ours."

We sold to people along the way—miners, operators, and everybody. They saw us coming with that old mule and they came running out: "Hey, hey, whatcha got there? Sure, I'll take some of this! Yeah, gimme some of that too!"

Grandma Mary couldn't read or write. She never went to school, but she still did a good business because she could count. She never weighed anything. She measured it all out in two buckets, a gallon and a peck, hung on the side of that mule. Grandma knew a gallon from a peck. She knew a quarter from a dollar, too.

We carried our stuff to U. G. Browning's store in Barnabus and sold him eggs, smoked hams, and bacon. Grandma Mary always bought me candy there, and we bought some for my little sister, too.

As the years went by, it got harder for Tommy and Grandma Mary to get in and out of Cow Creek, especially of a wintertime. So they bought themselves a place in Barnabus. They spent their winters there—like the way some people go to Florida now.

The Curry house in Barnabus was painted yellow. At that time, it was the only painted house in town, which really made it stand out. In the summertime, as soon as Mary and I rode around the curve, Grandma started bragging on that place.

"Lookie yonder, Raymond," she said. "There's our pretty house!"

"Yeah, Grandma, I like it too."

These were the rituals of my life: gardening, canning, and peddling with Grandma Mary. And it all came together on Decoration Day.

It came in the spring of the year. People came from all around to put flowers on the family graves. The ivy bloomed full of honeysuckle, and different wildflowers grew. All orange, peach, purple, and blue—the prettiest things you ever saw.

Decoration—Memorial—Day was held at three cemeteries: one at Barnabus, where most of my dad's people are buried; another down at the Melvin Farley place; and one at Uncle Victor's, the Curry cemetery. The first Sunday, they had Decoration Day in Barnabus, where there was more sunshine, and the flowers bloomed the soonest. Then they'd have it at the Farley place the next week. Finally, they'd have one at Uncle Victor's.

All of Victor's people came in for Decoration Day, and all of ours came too. People arrived in their wagons and buggies from miles around. So many wagons came it was hard to find a place to park them all—along the road, down by the fishing pond.

They had church all day, with eight or ten preachers getting up to preach and sing, preach and sing. People laid their wildflowers on the graves, and sometimes they had paper ones they'd made. Best of all, though, was the food.

Some of the women came a day or two beforehand to cook. Chickens were killed and cans of meat were opened up. By the time everyone else got there to decorate, our big kitchen table was all laid out. The family came and sat at that table with milk, meat, butter, and honey—all the food they'd raised themselves—and they had themselves a meal.

Some years, when they got a great big crowd, dinner was served "on the ground." Sheets were spread at the cemetery like a giant picnic. It was the only time I ever got any ice. One coal-company store put an ice plant in at Omar, and the men went down there to get us blocks of ice. They wrapped those blocks in quilts, blankets, and brown tarpaulins. They brought it up, and we'd get to eat that ice.

Some of the young ones slipped off to dance. Decoration was a way of getting a family's girls "married off." The girls all dressed the best they could and met new boyfriends when they came in for Decoration.

Sometimes people stayed all night, sleeping on the porch or wherever they could. Of course, that tickled us kids to death to get to sleep on the porch of a summertime. Throw us down a quilt or something, or we'd wrap ourselves up in one of those wool army blankets from World War I. Even outdoors, you could roll up in one of those blankets and sweat all night.

If you can't follow all my relations, no matter. If it's a Curry or a Chafin, you can pretty much figure that I'm related to it somehow. The point is this: all my uncles and aunts were the people around Cow Creek and Logan County who helped get me started. I grew up being around all these people all the time, and that got me to liking them—and them to liking me. Growing up, they brought me candy and did things for me. I was close to them, and I felt I owed them a lot. I was always friendly to everyone, so when I started getting into politics, I was always with the family when they needed me. They always stood by me; and when I got to where I could help them, I stood by them too.

2 Appalachian Spring

WHEN I WAS FIVE OR SIX YEARS OLD, MY family moved out of Cow Creek and into Barnabus. We lived in a company place, less than two hundred feet from that "pretty yellow house" my Grandma Mary loved so much. She and Tommy had moved in there one winter and never did go back to Cow Creek.

Barnabus was thick with houses then—most of it private property, not company land. The Brownings had bought it from the Currys and sold it off in lots, so the town was about the only place where you could build a store or anything like that. Two Browning brothers, Wayne and U. G., each owned a "general merchandise" store, where they sold different things—groceries, hardware, dry goods, shoes, and things like that.

Barnabus had a restaurant run by a black family named Berman. Mrs. Berman was the best cook in the world, that old lady was. I was in third or fourth grade when she cooked hotdogs on weekends and sold them from a tent to people up on Pine Creek. An Italian family, the DeFobios, ran a big bakery just below my grandparents' place. I guess I wasn't but five years old the first time I walked by that bakery with my mother and smelled that good bread baking.

"Mmmm, what's that smell, Mommy?"

"That's someone makin' bread, honey," she said. "That's a bakery. One of these days, we'll buy us a fresh loaf of bread in there."

Barnabus had one church, the Holiness Church. (Some of us called it the "holy-roller church" back then.) Laura Curry was the preacher. She had red hair and a temperament to match. Laura shot and killed her first husband and then married one of my great-uncle Victor Curry's sons. She came clear of the shooting—never served any time for it—but some of our people still never took to her too well. My grandmother liked her, though, because Laura was a good neighbor, always baking things and giving us stuff.

Laura's second husband, Harley, had the only taxi in our area and he ran the first bus line out of here. We were neighbors and everybody got up early then, about five or six in the morning. When one of his buses wouldn't start, Harley asked my daddy to hook one or two of his horses up to pull-start it. I fed the horses every morning, and when Harley got one of those taxis started, he gave me a ride to the railroad crossing. Then I'd walk back home.

Barnabus had a saloon in those days, the Blue Goose, right at the mouth of Cow Creek. The Blue Goose was a real big club with slot machines, poker rooms, and a bar. It had a restaurant out front, a barber shop, and bedrooms upstairs. I don't think there was ever any honkey-tonkin' going on up there, though. A woman might go into the Blue Goose for a drink, but Tennis Hatfield ran it as a club for men. A man could take his wife and kids into the restaurant, and they'd be treated with respect there.

Prohibition was a fact in West Virginia long before the rest of the country voted for it, but Tennis Hatfield could still sell liquor at the Blue Goose. The county sheriff, Don Chafin, was his first cousin. Don didn't let anyone sell liquor but Tennis. Other people could always slip around and sell it, but nobody besides Tennis ran a saloon. Tennis and his brother Joe were politicians just like Don—except the Hatfields later became Republicans.

I was real young when Don Chafin had his political heyday in Logan County. We were never political enemies, but we were never political friends either. We were related, but distantly so. The first thing Don Chafin did when he came in here, I believe, was work for the county assessor. Later he ran for that job and, from there, he got himself elected sheriff. His power eventually grew to where he could run the elections and dictate who succeeded him.

Coal was going strong back then in the early twenties. There must have been fifteen mines just on this one creek alone, and no one man owned two of them. Mine operators and owners came in from all over the place—from New York and Cincinnati and other places. They came to Logan on the trains and Harley Curry was always at the station with one of his taxis. They climbed into his cab and Harley drove them around to see their mines. While they looked at their operations and talked with their foremen, Harley waited. Some of them paid him all day long, just to drive around and wait on them.

Harley also took a lot of those operators up to the Blue Goose, where they could do just about anything they wanted. They might have a drink or two, and if one of them took one too many, Tennis Hatfield and his bartenders helped that man upstairs. He might sleep it off at the Blue Goose, or Harley might taxi him back down to the Aracoma Hotel in Logan.

Sheriff Don Chafin was kind of like a king to those operators. He dressed real good and he treated them royally, too. He was always real glad to see them. He liked to see them open up their mines because they paid him to keep things under control for them. Whenever those coal operators came to Logan County, one of Don's men always protected them, if they needed it.

Don was an accommodating man. If he knew someone who wasn't able to work in the mines and needed a job, he tried to help him. He went to a mine superintendent or a coal owner, saying, "I've got a fellow here who can't work right now. I want you to hire him as a deputy," and they'd let that man work a year or so as a night watchman around the mines. The county didn't pay those deputies. Don paid them money that came from the coal companies. People figured that Don Chafin wasn't taking as much from the taxpayers that way. That's part of what made him so popular.

Eventually, Don had one or two mine guards at just about every mine and precinct. All of them had police power, same as any deputy, and many of them were Don's political workers, too. That's how his political machine operated. Don controlled his people. He made sure they helped folks. If one of his men got drunk, fooled around, or didn't do his job, Don Chafin fired that man and put in another one.

When he ran an election, Don went to the coal operator again. He might tell one, say, in Omar, "You're gonna pay me five hundred dollars to work this precinct. I need five hundred dollars for it." And they gave him that money to organize that precinct. Another company might have given him four hundred dollars for a precinct that wasn't as big. But they all paid him to hire his drivers and do whatever he needed to get the votes to win. That's the way he kept his power back then.

Whenever the operators found somebody agitating for the union and aggravating them, Don used the law to protect their companies. After World War I, the United Mine Workers started sending more organizers in here, putting one over at this mine and another over there. Pretty soon, they had enough men to get up a little crowd and they started organizing a mine or two. Just as soon as a coal operator heard anything about it, he told Don Chafin, and Don's deputies at the mine would start working on that union man. First thing you know, they'd catch him with something—moonshine, maybe—and that fellow was in trouble. Those deputies soon made him forget all about the union. Don had a lot of deputies back then—some three hundred of them during the Blair Mountain war.

The Blair Mountain war was a time when the miners decided they just *had* to get the union in here—and that's when all the "fun" started. The union leaders realized that they were getting their rear ends kicked in Logan and Mingo counties, so they started their big drive. In August 1921, a bunch started out from Charleston and tried to march through Logan to Mingo County. By the time they reached Blair Mountain, there were thousands of them.

Don Chafin heard about it and started bringing in carloads of volunteers, machine guns, and rifles. He hired a couple of airplane pilots to fly around and watch what was going on—and they even dropped homemade bombs on the miners.

While these thousands of union miners were marching toward Logan, Don got up before the crowd there and said, "Boys, they want to come in here and take us out! They want to control everything—shut us down and blow up our mines! Are you ready?"

"Yeah," they said. "We ain't gonna let them do it! We'll fight!"

When the miners got close to Blair, Don's people—I don't know how many thousands of them—were waiting at the top of the ridge. From Logan to Main Island Creek, men and guns were loaded onto flatcars and hauled up to Ethel, near the mountain. Anybody who signed on got a rifle. You'd have thought they were fighting World War II up there! Eventually,

President Warren Harding sent two thousand U.S. soldiers in—and a squad of bombing planes—and both sides backed down.

A lot of men fought for Don Chafin on Blair Mountain, but after the union came, they were afraid to tell it. It must have been a pretty big battle back then. I don't know how many men got killed up there.[1]

I had two cousins who told me all about it. Cecil Chafin was eleven or twelve and his brother was four or five years older at the time, I believe. Cecil and his brother liked guns—and they just worshipped Don Chafin. Cecil told me that they got near one of those trains going up to Blair and crawled on board, right in among the men on one of those flatcars. When somebody handed out the guns, one of the boys reached between somebody's legs and got himself one. They went up there and fought for about four or five days, bang-bang-bang, everywhere. People say the battlefront was twenty miles long.

Finally, one of the sergeants came around and found my cousins in the middle of it all. Cecil said those men brought them down the mountain, and Don Chafin took their gun away from them. Don sent them home, but not before he'd kicked their tail ends good.

I think it was sometime after the Blair Mountain war when Don Chafin started getting big money from the coal operators. He told me he got fifty cents for every carload of coal that came out of this valley. He said he told the owners, "If you want me to keep the union out, it's fifty cents a car." You can imagine how many hundreds of railroad cars went out of here every day. I don't know how long that lasted, but that's what he got.

Don didn't like the union, but he didn't let those coal companies just kick the miners around any way they wanted to. He didn't let them thump the workers and make them dig coal in

---

1. Accounts of fatalities still differ, but one historian, Lon Savage, in *Thunder in the Mountains: The West Virginia Mine War, 1920–21* (Pittsburgh: University of Pittsburgh Press, 1990), puts the number at less than twenty.—T. S.

water holes, the way some of these nonunion mines do today. They didn't have the mud coming over the tops of their shoes and working in unsafe conditions, like some of them are now. By the 1930s, when the union had come in big, Don Chafin had seen the writing on the wall: He ran a coal mine at Peach Creek—and it was a union operation.

When his term expired, Don ran his brother-in-law for sheriff. That's what caused the Hatfields to get into it with him. Tennis, Don's first cousin, especially, didn't like the deal. He wanted to run himself for sheriff. Tennis fell out with Don, became a Republican, and started getting some power, cutting Don Chafin out. Their political fighting eventually got both of them in trouble. They got to squawking on each other, and everything came out about the Blue Goose. Don was sent to federal prison on a prohibition conviction, and Tennis got some jail time too. The whole thing was kind of like a married couple getting into it: Everything comes out and they both lose. That's what happened to the Chafins and the Hatfields.[2]

I started school in 1924, when I was seven years old. The Barnabus Grade School had two rooms, where they taught kids up to the fifth or sixth grade. My sister, Bessie, was a little younger than me, but we started school together that year. They were teaching the primer.

In the last part of 1924, things got bad. As it was, our family didn't have a whole lot, but a mine fire forced the Number Four Mine at Omar to shut down, putting my dad out of work. That winter, we moved back to Cow Creek and farmed there the following spring. Bessie and I stopped going to school then because it was too far to walk.

2. I should say here that I get along pretty good with the Hatfields today. There's two of them living up on Island Creek—two of Tennis's boys—and we get along fine with each other.—R. C.

Later, my dad heard about a railroad being built up Pine Creek, three miles away. They were putting in about five miles of rail line from Omar to a mine at the head of the creek owned by the Island Creek Coal Company. My daddy thought he'd get back into hauling lumber for the bridges and everything they needed to build up there, so we moved to Pine Creek in the winter of 1924–25.

At Pine Creek, Bessie and I started school again. Both of us had been promoted to the third grade, mostly because of the work our mother had done with us at home; we'd gotten through the primer and the first two readers with her.

Things went pretty well after that. My daddy got back into the timber business, cutting and selling ceiling props for the mines. He hired men to cut and split the timber, and they cut three or four miles up Pine Creek. At the same time, he was hauling sawed lumber for the Peytona Lumber Company, material they were selling for the railroad construction.

He hauled other things, too, that year—cement, sand, and gravel for the railroad bridges and culverts. When there wasn't school, I worked with him. Fathers did that back then. They took their boys everywhere, and young people learned to work that way. My dad and I loaded lumber onto our wagon at the Peytona lumber mill and hauled it to the construction sites on Pine Creek. I even went around with him to some of the deep mines—at least to the ones where they'd let me go.

I was only eight or nine years old then, but that was plenty old enough for me to drive a team. My daddy had long since taught me how to drive. I sat with him in that high spring seat while he taught me how to do it. As we came down steeper hills, he pulled on the break rope near the driver's side. He held that rope down with his foot, locking the rear wheels of the wagon, and guided us down the hill. The first time I asked to hold the brake, my daddy said no; he said I might fall off and get run over. The bigger I got, though, the more he trusted me. That was really something, when he let me hold that brake.

We were still living on Pine Creek at the end of 1926 when a man named Art Chambers was killed, over in Rum Creek. Art Chambers, who had been one of Don Chafin's toughest deputies, was married to a woman named Cynthia Raines. She and Art were the parents of my wife, Louise.

Cynthia Raines was a schoolteacher. Before she married Art, she taught school at the head of Cow Creek. Every week, she walked over a hill to Chauncey, across the river to the mouth of Rum Creek, across another hill, and down to Barnabus, where somebody met her with a horse to take her up the hollow. She boarded up there for the week—just like Louise did later, when I first met her. Cynthia taught all my aunts and uncles and my mother, too. (My mother never did quit after she learned to read and write. She studied a lot of things on her own. She read history and she was good in math. She was the best educated one of all her family.)

When they were married, Art and Cynthia Chambers lived at Dehue on Rum Creek. They lived there until Louise was about eight years old. That was when Art got to drinking, fighting, and causing some trouble. He and Cynthia separated and were in the process of getting a divorce when Art got into an election-day scrape over politics. That was 1926, when the Hatfields were just taking things over from Don Chafin.

It was during the August primary, and Art Chambers was working the election ground at Yolyn for Don's faction. The way we heard it, the Hatfields had it in for Art's father, who was a political leader on Rum Creek. The Hatfields figured that this was their time to move in on things. Howard Searls was part of it; he'd been talking about it to people.

"That Chambers gang has been running things to suit themselves for a long time," someone heard him say.

Art's father was working inside the election house—the polling place—and Art was outside when the Hatfields' people drove up. They had a big truckload of men, fellows who used to live at Yolyn but had since moved away. The story goes that the Hatfields were hauling these men from one precinct to another, getting them into the polls to vote Republican.

When this bunch pulled in to vote at Yolyn, though, Art Chambers spoke up about it, saying they didn't belong in that precinct. Art got into it with Searls and another fellow, and somebody shot him. Art fell onto his knees and he started to get back up. Then one of those fellows shot him in the head. They tried Searls and the other man for murder, and Searls got fifteen years. I think later he was pardoned for the crime; I don't think he ever really served any time for it. The other man was found not guilty and he never served any time, either.

There were a lot of shootings around Logan back then. I remember one the very next summer, when I was ten years old. A whole lot of people were moonshining and bootlegging in those days. Grandpa Tommy Curry had died, but Grandma Mary lived at the mouth of the left fork of Cow Creek, and we went to visit her there pretty often. That was when I saw and heard a good deal about the killings of Chauncey Holler.[3]

Tennis Hatfield had won the sheriff's office by then, and it was like any other administration; if you were "in good" with them, you had nothing to worry about. You could bootleg and do whatever you wanted to. If you didn't get with the Hatfields, though, you pretty much had to keep looking over your shoulder.

There still weren't too many Republicans in Chapmanville, though, and the Hatfields had to give those few some kind of a

---

3. Raymond's account of this shooting is supplemented with material from the *Logan Banner* of that time.

job if they wanted to stay on top of things in Logan County. Ed Hensley was one of Chapmanville's Republicans. I don't know if he asked for it or not, but the Hatfields made Ed a state revenue agent, and then they turned him loose.

Hensley had himself a big family, and a lot of them were ginseng diggers. He'd take them out into the woods of a weekend and they'd just wander around until they came across a bed of ginseng, or somebody with a still. If it was ginseng, his family dug it up; if it was a still, Hensley reported it to the Hatfields, or he'd arrest them sometimes on his own. But he was an independent man and he made damned sure that those stills were torn up. Usually, the Hatfields controlled everything, telling their boys to go bother so-and-so, and to leave so-and-so alone. But apparently they lost control over their man Hensley because he had a reputation of tearing up stills wherever he could find them.

Some fellows from Chauncey Holler—Mitt and Bird Nelson, Millard Porter, and Isom Curry—were moonshining over in Miller's Fork, working at least three stills up there. The Nelson bunch was "in" with the Hatfields, so they pretty much had a license to moonshine up that hollow. They figured that no state or federal revenue man was going to come bother them because the Hatfields' connections reached all the way to Charleston. The Nelsons had everything they needed to make their moonshine whiskey. They even had a little shanty where they did their own cooking.

So, Hensley and his crew went up Chauncey Holler one day, just walking and a-ginsenging up there. They say that Ed was kind of nervy and wore his federal badge for everyone to see. The bootleggers got wind of the fact that he was getting near their place. Millard Porter, Bird Nelson, and his father, Sherman Nelson, went down to see what was going on.

"Hey there!" one of the Nelsons said. "This is our holler! You better get your damned asses out of here! You're gonna get yourselves killed!"

Now I knew some of these Chapmanville people and you couldn't tell them anything. You sure couldn't just run them out of a place like that, so Hensley and his bunch told themselves, "It's a bunch of hot air. Piss on 'em." They went back up there the next day—right near the Nelsons' hiding place.

This time, the group was met by Isom Curry, Millard Porter, and both Nelson boys. Isom had gotten to within four or five feet of the Hensleys when Mitt yelled for the revenuer and his family to throw up their hands. Hensley wasn't having any.

"You goddamned bootleggers!" he yelled. "We got guns too, and we can take care of you!"

By God, those Nelsons and Isom Curry started shooting. One of Hensley's boys got hit in the chest and another took a bullet in the back. They say Isom shot Hensley himself through the head. One other fellow was hit too, but he got away to tell about it.

Right off, Tennis Hatfield set to looking for the Nelsons. He had more than thirty men hunting around Cow Creek, figuring that Isom Curry, being related to everyone up here, would turn up first. But those boys didn't show up in Cow Creek that night. Actually, I think they waited until later on.

Eventually, they caught Isom Curry and Millard Porter. Those boys had laid out in the woods someplace, practically starving themselves for a week, before coming out of the hills. Isom and Millard were blamed for the whole thing, and I believe they went to the penitentiary. Sherman Nelson, the boys' father, was charged with something, but the jury let him go.

Mr. Nelson was a friend of my dad's. My father had bought moonshine off of him, and Mr. Nelson stayed overnight with us sometimes in Maysburg. One day, years after all this had blown over, Mr. Nelson and my father were talking about it together, and I heard Mr. Nelson say something about the Hatfields sending their men up there to kill his boys.

My dad agreed with him. He said he didn't think the Hatfields had any interest in arresting them. They didn't want those Nelsons coming out of there alive. The Hatfields would just as soon have bushwhacked every one of them. After all, the Nelsons and Isom Curry could have told people a thing or two, and the Hatfields didn't want the story to get out—not if they could help it.

On the other hand, maybe the Hatfields didn't mind letting Mitt and Bird Nelson go. I'm sure they were afraid the whole political deal would come out. But they never did find those Nelson boys, and I figure they must have gotten help from someone—probably somebody on Cow Creek. They got free of here, and nobody ever heard from them again after that.

That same year, in 1927, my dad bought himself his first truck. It was a big black Ford, with a bed that could carry fifteen or sixteen big mine props at a load. It was fine machine, although my mother wasn't too much for it.

"I don't know what in the world you want with that!" she told him. "You can't even drive it!"

But my daddy said it didn't matter; he'd figure it out. He did, too. He took that truck up and down the creek and nearly splashed every mud hole dry learning how to drive that thing. He got real good at it.

"Well, Mrs. Chafe," he said, "We're gonna really make us some money now!"

But my mother wasn't so sure about that. She told him she was going to keep feeding the horses; they were less likely to break down.

My daddy's brother worked as a car salesman. He must have been pretty good at it because, by 1928 or '29, he'd sold my daddy another truck. Then things got bad. The coal mines weren't doing well, the stock market crashed, and we fell behind on the payments. One evening, at the dinner table, my mother delivered the bad news.

"There was a constable up here about those trucks," she said. My dad didn't think much of it.

"Aw, they can't take 'em," he said.

But he was wrong about that. A couple of days later, a big constable and two other men came looking at that brand-new truck. There it was, sitting right out in front of the house. They asked my mother where the other one was.

"It's out yonder, in the barn," she told them.

They had a gasoline can with them, and they poured gas into each tank. Then they drove both those trucks right out of here, back to Logan.

My dad had been out that day, probably looking at some timber. He came home later, and it really broke him up to lose those trucks. He never did get them back. The worst thing about it was that he'd gone ahead and sold almost all of his horses. There was nothing left for him to do but go back into the mines. Almost overnight, our family had been hit by the Depression.

3 Work and Politics

SOMETIME AFTER HE LOST HIS TRUCKS, MY daddy went to work loading coal in the Number Five Mine at Omar. It was nothing new to him; he'd done it before. But working in a coal mine isn't much like working out in the woods. Loading coal underground doesn't compare to cutting and hauling timber outdoors. My daddy didn't like the mines at all.

Eventually, though, he got himself a new contract, an outside job, unloading slate—"mine refuse"—at fifty cents a car. Before long, he had a team of his own to run that slate, and he was hiring men to work with him. Then the company installed an automated slate dump at the mine, and that put all of them out of work again.

One day, a friend of my daddy's came along and told him, "Elbert, you damn-near killed yourself runnin' that slate anyway. I'll give you two dollars and forty cents a day to work on the coal tipple for me."

So my father—I called him "Poppy" then—went down there and ran the "slat cars," which carried the graded coal from the tipple down to the trains. It was easy, but it was dirty, nasty work.

He worked up to sixteen hours a day for that two-forty, and he stayed just long enough to get himself another job.

That one came from my mother's brother, who got him hired to drive the delivery wagon for the Junior Mercantile, a company store at Omar. The Junior Mercantile was owned by the same outfit that ran the West Virginia Coal and Coke Company, and the Omar store was the main one among a whole chain of them.

Every store back then had a delivery wagon and a horse—or maybe two or three—to deliver the groceries to people. It wasn't like today where you just go in, pick out what you want, and leave with it. You went into that store and told them what you needed—a bag of flour, a pound of beans, or three boxes of salt—and the clerks took your order back to the ware room. They boxed that stuff up while you went on your way and, later, they delivered it to your house. The store drivers ran on a schedule, and it might be nine or ten o'clock in the evening before you got your groceries, but everything came right to your front door. Junior Mercantile had one team of horses and my daddy was hired to run that team and carry things to customers around Omar.

My daddy loved taking care of the Junior Mercantile's horses, and he was good at it, too. He curried those animals every day, and he'd shine those harnesses, the ones with the big knobs sticking up. He made those teams look real good—better than most people keep their cars today—and the company liked him. They called him "the horse man."

Eventually, my daddy got to do about anything a person could do for that store. He cut meat, sold furniture, and worked in the stockroom. He could do any of it, and they paid him up to $135 a month, which was pretty good money in the thirties around here.

I was going to the junior high school in Omar during the day, but in the evenings I was right there with my daddy, watching him and helping work in that store. As time went on, the company decided to put in a big bowling alley at the Junior Mercantile, and he saw this as a good chance for me to get a regular job. He went to the managers and told them he wanted his boy to work in that bowling alley.

"He's awful little," they said, looking me over.

"That don't matter," my daddy told them. "How much would you pay him?"

They offered a dollar a night for me to work from four to midnight, six hours' work, and Poppy told them that'd be fine with me.

"I'll pick you up after school tomorrow," he said. "I'll bring you home and get your supper; then you come back up here and work in the bowling alley. It won't hurt you none."

"OK, Poppy," I said. I'd sure never worked in a bowling alley before, but I was game for anything.

By God, I got up there and made seven dollars a week—working every day, setting up those pins and rolling the balls back to the bowlers from behind the frames. There were three of us setting up the pins, lickety-split, one-two-three, and none of us hardly had time to stop. They didn't have automatic pinsetters like they do now, or air conditioning. Buddy, it got real hot working back there.

One day, the manager got the idea of paying us by the game. Instead of a dollar a night, he started paying us five cents a game to set up those pins. But the plan backfired on him. Me and my friends set up the pins and rolled those balls back as fast as a chicken pickin' up corn. Each of us started making a dollar and a quarter, sometimes a dollar and a half a night. Of course, the manager got tired of the new deal and cut us back to a dollar a night; but that was still fine with me.

On Saturdays, I helped my dad deliver groceries. By that time the Junior Mercantile had a truck, and we drove to company stores all over the place in Lyburn, Rossmore, Monaville, Chauncey, Micco. There were at least ten stores, all in places where West Virginia Coal and Coke had mines, and they all fed out of a warehouse in Barnabus near our store at Omar.

The general manager over all these stores was T. A. Obenshain, a man I came to love and respect as much as any of my own family. Mr. Obenshain had only one arm, and I helped him carry his own groceries to his house on a hill. I worked in the Obenshains' yard, cut grass around their flower beds, and Mr. Obenshain usually gave me a quarter or fifty cents—sometimes a dollar for the work I did. I thought that man could walk on water, he was such a nice old fellow. His wife was a fine woman too, and they had a couple of girls who were well educated. They taught school and were as good to me as their parents were.

My family lived up the Left Fork of Cow Creek at the time, and almost everybody up there sold moonshine. Now, my dad never did sell a drop of liquor in his life, but he did deliver it to people: Dr. Smith, Dr. Hederman, general mine superintendent Joe Korbly—all those fellows. He came to know everyone around here real well—the doctors, mine operators, and everybody—because he delivered their moonshine. When he carried groceries around someplace, he usually took a gallon or two along with him, and a superintendent or a doctor would give him maybe two or three dollars for a gallon. They trusted my daddy. They knew he only carried the good kind. And a lot of the best moonshiners up and down this creek liked him, too, because he got them *cash*. Poppy never made any money off of it, but he sure made a lot of friends.

I'm gonna tell this "little one" on my dad and Mr. Obenshain. Every year at Christmas, the Junior Mercantile stores bought turkeys for its stores and it was our job at Omar to get those turkeys brought in. One day, Mr. Obenshain came out into the store where my daddy was.

"By golly, Elbert," he said. "Every year we send somebody out to get those turkeys for us. Let's you and me go get them this time!"

"Where's that?" my daddy asked.

"Monroe County," the old man said.

Now, my daddy had never traveled very far from Logan County. He'd been as far as Charleston maybe one time in his entire life, and he'd been over into Kentucky to buy some horses, but that's about it. When Mr. Obenshain suggested they drive to Monroe County together, Poppy jumped at the chance. I was working at the store then, and I couldn't help but overhear all of this. After Mr. Obenshain left, I asked my dad whether I could go along.

"Hot-damn! Get out of here, boy!" he said. "You know you can't go with us!"

Later, Mr. Obenshain came around and he saw that I was unhappy.

"What's the matter with you, Sonny?" he said.

"I asked Poppy if I could go with you to Monroe County, and he said 'no.' "

Mr. Obenshain sided right up with my dad.

"Hell no, you can't go!" he said. And that pretty much dropped my feathers altogether. I figured that was that.

Later, I was just coming back from making some deliveries when Mr. Obenshain called me over to him.

"Sonny," he said, laying his hand on my shoulder. "Would you like to ride with the truck driver to get those turkeys?"

He knew I did.

"Go over to the dry-goods store," he said. "Pick you out some clothes—get you some good ones—and we'll let you ride in that truck."

"But Poppy said I couldn't go," I told him.

"By God, I'll handle 'Poppy'! You just leave it to me!" (Afterward, I figured that one of Mr. Obenshain's daughters had talked him into letting me go.)

Mr. Obenshain and my father left ahead of time in a company car, a brand-new Dodge. (Chrysler Corporation bought most of the coal around here, so the mining officials used nothing but Dodges and Plymouths.) The next day, I left in a big two-ton truck with Ham Jones, a black fellow who worked in the store with us.

It took us all day to get that truck to Monroe County. We arrived at the turkey farm just before dark, and I never did see such a place. That farmer had a big grandstand, just like at a baseball game, with turkeys roosting all over it. There must have been hundreds of turkeys on that thing. We'd been there a while when Old Man Obenshain turned to the farmer.

"Well," he said, "Where's my driver and this boy gonna sleep?"

Just then, the man's wife stepped out on the porch, saying, "Ain't no nigger gonna sleep in my house!"

Old Man Obenshain didn't know what to do. He'd already bought those turkeys, already written a check for them. Ham spoke up.

"It's all right," he said. "I'll just sleep in the truck."

I told them I'd sleep there too. So Ham and I bedded down for the night in the back of the two-ton truck.

Let me tell you, it was a good thing we didn't stay in that house, because we wouldn't have gone to sleep in there, no ways. Three other buyers were on that farm, and all of them just partied and danced all night long. My dad and Mr. Obenshain got about as drunk as two hoot owls, and so did the rest of them there.

The next morning, Ham and I loaded the turkeys and

made the trip back to Logan County. I figured Poppy and Mr. Obenshain were nursing some pretty good headaches on their way home.

Two or three weeks later, I was standing on the back porch of the Junior Mercantile store when a big truck pulled in—just as big as a moving van. Darned if that thing wasn't full of walnuts—whole black English walnuts—more than a hundred bushels of them! The driver walked up, and I recognized him as the owner of the Monroe County turkey farm.

"Goddamn!" I said to him. "Where you goin' with all those walnuts?"

"Mr. Obenshain and your dad bought 'em," the man said.

I found Mr. Obenshain in his office. "The man you bought them turkeys from is here," I said. "He's got your walnuts."

"By God, boy!" he growled. "What walnuts?"

He went out there and saw that truck for himself.

"You got these for us?" he asked the farmer.

"Yeah!" the man said. "You even paid me for them. I just cashed the check."

About that time, my daddy walked up, and Mr. Obenshain was heated up pretty good.

"Goddammit, Elbert," he said. "I ought to fire you! Why the hell'd you let me buy all these damned walnuts?"

Shoot, Poppy didn't know. He'd been just as drunk as Obenshain the night they bought those nuts. He'd forgotten about them too.

There was nothing to be done about it, though. They called in five or six extra people and hunted up every box and bushel basket they could find. We loaded those walnuts into the basement, except for a few jars that went on display in the store. But there was no way they'd sell. Everybody had walnuts. They grew all over the place around here.

One day an old fellow came into the store at Omar, a regular customer who lived in a place we called Seven-Hundred Hill.

His name was Alshire, and he took care of about a dozen grandchildren—all of them kids his children had left him. Mr. Alshire had been injured somehow, unable to work, and he owed our store three or four hundred dollars, which was a whole lot of money back then.

"I'm sorry, Mr. Alshire," said Mr. Obenshain. "Truly, I can't carry you no more. I've just got to cut you off. . . ."

My daddy was standing there, listening, and he spoke up.

"You know, Mr. Obenshain," he said. "We might sell some of these walnuts better if we had them cracked. Mr. Alshire here has all them kids where he lives—some great-big boys and girls. . . ."

Mr. Obenshain turned to his customer.

"What would you want for crackin' a bushel of walnuts?" he asked.

"I don't know," Alshire answered. "Just take what you can off my bill."

Pretty soon, I was loading walnuts onto the wagon and taking them up Seven-Hundred Hill, where the old man and those kids set to cracking. They used hammers, stove irons, and whatever else they could find to crack those whole black English walnuts. They put them in fruit jars and we took them back to the store.

It got to be a regular thing, me taking the walnuts up there and the old man and those kids working away, cracking nuts. I don't know how many quart-jars Mr. Obenshain got out of those people, but he sold every one of them in the store. Later, he called that turkey farmer back and ordered up a whole new load.

Sometime after that, my dad got sick. His sickness confined him to bed most of the time. I'd been working at Junior Mercantile for a good while by then, and he'd taught me a lot about how things worked. I was driving the truck even before I was old enough to get an operator's card. The day I turned sixteen, I got my license and Old Man Obenshain hired me to drive the company truck, just like my dad.

Two other men worked there along with me—Bill Parks and his brother Ted, two black men. Their mother worked in the Omar Drug Store cooking meals for all the company officials who could afford to buy them. After my dad got sick, I didn't have much money for lunch, so Mrs. Parks—"Miss Lynn" I called her—always fixed me something to eat. She called me to the back of the drugstore, where she fixed me out a plate of fried chicken or fish. And she never charged me a dime. Sometimes she even fixed me something to take home to my daddy; Miss Lynn was like a mother to me.

We didn't have all the hatred back then that we have now. Many was the weekend that Ted and Bill Parks went hunting with me and my father. We camped out, cooked ribs on the fire, and laughed together as we shared a jar of moonshine. There were days when the rain came down and flooded our creek to where I couldn't make it home. I'd go straight to Bill Parks's place and he gave me supper; I stayed all night and got breakfast there, too.

You see, the coal companies brought people of all nationalities and backgrounds together here in Logan County. They segregated a lot of the neighborhoods, but all the miners' houses were basically the same. Incomes were closer together, too. You might have one family with four hundred dollars and another with two hundred; but you didn't have it like it is today—one family with a million and this one over here with nothing. When a person died, there were as many black people at the funeral as there were white. Nothing like the fighting you have today.

The more I worked, the more I got to be like my dad. I could work just about anywhere in that store. I liked the dry goods department; didn't care for hardware much. Of course, people were still making a lot of things for themselves in those days—furniture and so on—but I could sell it too. I could sell two- or three-thousand-dollars' worth of stuff in a single day—stoves, washing machines, couches, and the like. And, because I could drive, I even delivered them.

"Sonny," Mr. Obenshain told me one day, "You'll never be as good as your daddy, but you're damn-near close, so I'm raising your pay."

He hiked it up to more than four dollars a day, a real nice raise. I got to know more about how the company worked, and before long they made me a clerk. It got to be where they almost couldn't do without me.

I was a great-big boy in those days; I dressed pretty good, and I got along with everybody. In 1933, I bought myself a used car. It was a yellow 1924 Pontiac with a top that laid back and roll-up windows in the doors. It had wire-spoke wheels and two big spare tires that rode on the fenders, the prettiest car you ever laid your eyes on. Then I had some trouble.

One Sunday, when I was about eighteen years old, me and this other boy decided to ride down to the Grand Ole Opry, which was putting on three shows in Omar that day. He drove us over there for the first show, which was too crowded, and we didn't get there early enough for the second show either, so we went home and started in on a gallon of moonshine.

We decided to go to Island Creek, where I could get a piece I needed for my car, which was broken down. As we came back down the hill, we had an accident. My buddy's car hit another car coming the other way. We hit it head on. I was the worst one injured in our car. I'd been riding on the front passenger side and I got knocked around pretty bad. I broke my neck and both legs and had a skull fracture. At the hospital, they put in a metal plate that I wear in my head to this day. The doctors thought the damage to my eyes would be enough to blind me for life. They were wrong about that, but, as it was, I was laid up all summer long in Logan General Hospital.

It was worse in the other car, the one we'd hit. It belonged to a doctor from another county. He and his whole family had been riding in it, and his daughter was killed.

Eventually, I was able to go back to work. I'd been there about two weeks when Mr. Obenshain's boss, S. C. Pohe, came through our store for a visit. Mr. Pohe was a vice-president of Junior Mercantile, a big, heavy man from Cincinnati. He walked through our store, talking real tough—because he *was* tough. Most unfortunately for me, though, Mr. Pohe had been good friends with the doctor whose car we'd hit.

I'll never forget the sight of Old Man Pohe and Mr. Obenshain standing upstairs together and looking over the ground floor of that store. I'll never forget how Old Man Pohe saw me and pointed his finger down at me with a scowl on his face. I knew he was asking what the hell I was doing there. I was the boy who'd been drunk and in a car wreck. I knew then that my days at Junior Mercantile were numbered. In fact, I was fired that very same afternoon.

But Mr. Pohe didn't stop after he fired me. He talked to every coal-mine operator in this county and told them, "That boy's no good. He was in a car wreck. Don't give him a job," and they listened to him. I couldn't get a job around here to save my life. I was blackballed by all the companies around, and that included their stores, about the only work I'd known.

I don't need to tell you that my family had a rough time of it that fall. I'd been fired, and Poppy was sick in bed. My seven brothers and sisters were all still in school, and the Depression was still on. If it weren't for Bill Parks, I don't know what we would have done. Bill had always kept a garden on our land, along with a hog or two, and he just about kept us from starving that year. Every so often he and some others at the Mercantile secretly boxed up some groceries and carried them to our place for me and my family.

Then the federal relief program came out, and my mother was able to get a weekly four-dollar check. (The relief officials in Logan were all Republicans at the time, and they made sure you took that check to the stores they liked. U. G. Browning was the Republican in our neck of the woods, so he got all that government business.)

We stayed on relief until Franklin Roosevelt reorganized the program and raised the check to six dollars a week. Then he started the Works Progress Administration (WPA), which raised that check to $35.80 a month, but you had to work for it. Around here, the WPA built bridges and roads, put up flood walls, and things like that. My dad still not being able, I was the one in our family to go out and work for the WPA.

At the first, they had me sealing up old, abandoned coal mines. Aside from being dangerous in general, the old mines were a fine place to make moonshine—something the government didn't like. A lot of those places had plenty of water and everything you needed to make liquor. Our job was to seal up those old holes with rock walls so people couldn't get in there.

Every day I walked out of Cow Creek three-and-a-half miles to the mouth of the old Number Four Mine at Omar, the same mine where my daddy had scrapped the tram road some years before. I had to walk up and around these hills because there wasn't any road, and I didn't have a car, anyway. I had to wade the creeks and go around the hill every day—all for just $35.80 a month for my family.

There wasn't one single bridge across Cow Creek at the time—the road still went right up through the creek in several places—so they started another WPA project, building a new road with bridges. It made no sense for me to have to go all that way to the mine site, not when the government had a project right here in my own backyard. So a relative of mine—a WPA foreman—got me a transfer. They took me off the mine-sealing team and put me on the Cow Creek Road.

We set to that road with wheelbarrows, picks, and shovels. We carried rock, built walls, and graded the surface—all with hand tools. The first bridges we built were made of wood. They were good bridges, but those pole floors were rough. People had the awfulest time getting their horses across those poles, and a lot of times they just went around and drove their teams through the creek. Later, someone thought of throwing a little dirt on those bridges so the horses could walk easier across the poles.

The WPA laid about three or four miles of road up there, mostly by hand and wheelbarrows. I was young and stout in those days, and good with a sledgehammer. They used dynamite to shoot the rock out, and every hole for that dynamite had to be driven by hand.

We used a turn-drill and long-handled sledges, the way John Henry did. Three of us hammered on the same steel drill. I'd hit a lick, my buddy over here would hit a lick, and then the third fellow over there would hit one. A fourth man sat on a nail keg with both his hands on that drill. Every time one of us hit, he'd give that drill a twist. Every day we'd hit on that drill and he'd turn it every time. All of us were in rhythm hammering on that drill, bang-bang-bang, all day long.

4 1936: First Election

WE WERE ALL OF US YOUNG MEN THEN, my road crew and I were. But three or four other fellows who worked down below us a ways were even younger. We competed with them, each team trying to outdo the other.

"We nailed eight foot today!" we'd holler at them.

"Well, we got eleven!" they'd come back.

I remember one day sometime before the 1936 primary when it came my turn to fetch a bucket of drinking water over from the well. As I was drawing the bucket, I looked up to see George C. Steele standing there.

George Steele was a tall, handsome fellow in those days. He wasn't the Democratic chairman in Logan County; but he might as well have been for all the power he had. George had worked his way up from the mines, became a politician, and then started running a bunch of candidates of his own. He was a good manager, and he won most of his races. By 1936 George was a strong political boss, and he was stumping for Everett Workman, his candidate for sheriff and Logan's chief of police at the time.

George Steele stood there, watching me fill that water bucket, and he could see the big "WPA" painted on its side.

"Hey, Raymond, what are you doing with that?" he asked.

"I'm working for it," I said.

"You're on the relief?"

"Yeah."

Now, don't think it was easy for me to admit working for the WPA to George Steele. It really hurt my pride. It damn-near tore me up to have to be on relief, carrying those big rocks around on my shoulders and not making much of anything for it. I pictured the kids I'd gone to school with—them eating good and me not having a thing, them pointing their fingers: "Boy, look at that Raymond, working on the WPA." It hurt my pride but I'm telling you, when you're hungry you can't afford pride. I *had* to take relief; it was all there was, so I took it.

"You had yourself a good job over at the mercantile," George said. "What happened?"

I told him about the accident and about being blacklisted. He said it was too bad, and maybe he'd be able to help me out somehow.

"Tell you what I'll do," he said. "You've delivered groceries all up and down this creek. You know about everybody around here. I'll give you twenty dollars if you'll work for my faction on election day. You just go out, help people get in to vote and talk to them about Everett Workman.... You got a car?"

A car, hell. I had holes the size of silver dollars in the bottoms of my shoes—and them with pasteboards stuck in them, too. But George said that was no matter; I could still help, just by talking to folks when they got to the polls. I told him I'd do it. I really wanted that twenty dollars.

That night, I told my dad about it.

"I got me a job," I said.

"Doing what?"

1936: FIRST ELECTION

"I'm helping George Steele and Everett Workman in the primary. Mr. Steele said he'd give me twenty dollars."

"Hell no!" my old man thundered. "George Steele's a good feller, and you can work for whoever you want on election day! But you don't work in politics for no money! You sell your soul when you do that—and them not owing you nothing! You're selling your vote—and you don't do that! By God, I'm mad at George Steele for even offering you that twenty dollars!"

Then my mother jumped in.

"Now, Elbert," she said. "He was probably just trying to help...."

"That don't matter!" my dad said. "A man don't work for no money on election day!"

All this and I wasn't even old enough to vote yet! A few days later, George came up Cow Creek to visit some of his family. Apparently, he'd heard how angry Poppy had been, because he sent one of his relatives up to get me.

"Well, I hope Elbert didn't get too mad," George said when I got there. "I just wanted to help you out some."

He said he could see my father's side of things, but he still wanted me to work the election.

"You come down to the Barnabus precinct the first thing on election day," he said. "And maybe I can help you some other way."

Primary day rolled around. I got up real early and walked out of Cow Creek. I was the first one at the polls, long before the sun came up. The whole place was quiet, no one around—not an election officer or anybody. I waited there all by myself until some of the others showed up.

After the polls opened, of course, everybody who lived around there appeared. I helped George's people from 6:30 that morning to 7:30 that night. I got the vote out and campaigned for Everett Workman.

"Now, I know Everett," I told them. "And he's a good man! He's been chief of police for a long time...."

I didn't have a bite to eat that whole day long. At the end of it, after the polls closed, George's people started paying everybody. When they came around to me, I told them no.

"You don't owe me nothing," I said, and I walked back home.

After the primary, George Steele got me a laborer's job on the state road at forty cents an hour. Buddy, I was real proud of that job. I wanted people to see that I was working for the state road every day. Forty cents an hour! Boy, I was getting back up in the world!

Meanwhile, George and Everett were facing a much tougher fight in the general election. Everett could win against other Democrats; five or six others had run against him in the primary, and they had effectively split the vote. But he and George had a whole lot more trouble in the general for two reasons: First, the Republicans were still pretty strong in here back then—not like it is now; and, secondly, people up the creeks *hated* Everett Workman. They hated him because he was Logan's chief of police. They came into town to get drunk and fight, and Everett just threw them in jail. There wasn't hardly a weekend without his officers coming out and tossing some of them in jail overnight.

So when George sent Everett up some of these hollows to campaign, he was facing miners who didn't like him very much. There was usually some bunch that was half-drunk and wanted to fight him. They might start shoving Everett around, and then somebody would try to "pop" him one. It could have been dangerous for him, so George Steele decided that Everett needed a bodyguard.

In those days, I was a pretty mean fellow. I could swing a hammer just like John Henry, and I could fight real good, too. George figured I'd be just the man to guard Everett Workman during the primary, so I went off the WPA and started walking around with Logan's chief of police.

George also hired a couple of other fellows. One of them was Orville Hale—we called him "Butch"—a nice-looking fellow from a large political family. George chose Butch Hale because he had worked with me on the state road, and he'd been a boxer. Butch was a good scrapper, although he didn't nearly have the wind that I had.

As a "George Steele man," I stood real tall. They bought me some clothes—all the best—and they put us up at the Aracoma Hotel. We got all our meals for free at the Smoke House restaurant and just about anything else we wanted. George gave me a couple of guns too—two snub-nosed pistols—and I carried them around in my pockets.

They had everything in the world going on at the Aracoma Hotel and the Smoke House in those days—gambling, dice, and racetrack betting. I'd sure never seen such things. Hell, I wasn't even old enough to be in there, but nobody ran me out. I was a guard for Police Chief Everett Workman; the police sure weren't going to bother me, and nobody else was either.

"That's Everett Workman's man," they whispered. "One of George Steele's boys."

The time I spent in the Smoke House and the Aracoma Hotel amounted to "going to school" for me. But I never wanted to be a gambler. It just didn't appeal to me. I was happy just being a "George Steele man." I spent a lot of time with him and I liked him because George was real good to me. He had gotten me off relief and, every once in a while, he gave me extra pocket money. "Go buy yourself something," he said. George was like a father to me.

As the campaign went on, George had to fire a couple of Everett's bodyguards for drinking too much. (They drank to get up their nerve to fight. Some people are like that, but I never had to get my nerve up that way. If someone tried something with the man I was guarding, that was enough for me to let go on him.) With those firings, Butch and I were the only ones guarding Everett on this one particular evening when he was campaigning over on Coal River.

Now, Coal River in those days was the meanest damned place in the world. As I said before, the miners didn't think much of Everett Workman. Worse for me, though, the Coal River, near Sharples, was where the Blair Mountain war had started. The miners up there all remembered how Sheriff Don Chafin's deputies had gone up against their union in 1921. The name "Chafin" wasn't too well liked among them. So those men started getting into it with Everett Workman, pushing him around some, and pretty soon me and Butch had us a little skirmish on our hands.

We followed a plan we'd worked out before. Butch and I just pushed Everett through the crowd, into his car, and it drove off, getting the candidate out of the way. Unfortunately, that left me and Butch some distance from our own car. In order to get out of there, we had to fight our way back. I got knocked around pretty good—took some hard thumps on the head before we stumbled into that car, me behind the wheel. As I drove off, I noticed Butch breathing real heavy. "Goddamn, Butch!" I laughed. "You act like you're gonna die! You ought to do some training or something!"

In that 1936 election, Franklin Roosevelt had been in office for four years, and he was carrying a whole crowd of people over to the Democrats. That meant a lot to our campaign in Logan County, but it didn't make things easy for us. We had to campaign hard for Everett Workman. Aside from being unpopular in the coalfields, Everett was up against Ose Richey, a beer distributor and one tough Republican.

1936: FIRST ELECTION

Ose and his people had put posters up everywhere, and he campaigned from a big flatbed truck. Ose got around everyplace with that truck, all fixed up with a big band and lot of young girls riding on the back. That truck pulled into a town or a coal camp, and all kinds of people gathered around to watch Ose Richey step up to make his speeches.

"There's old Everett Workman!" he said. "Always putting you good fellers in jail every weekend! You elect me and I'll quit throwing you all in jail!"

Then the band would play and the girls would jump off that truck and pass out the buttons and literature: "OSE RICHEY FOR SHERIFF!"

Everett Workman didn't have a band or a truck, but he went around to the schoolhouses, where the political meetings were held. To tell the truth, Everett wasn't much of a speaker, but that was no matter. He was on the same side as FDR—and he had George Steele. This gets to a part of the story that taught me a big lesson about politics. I've always wanted to tell about it because it shows how things operated back then—and still do, to some extent.

George Steele, you'll remember, was the de-facto leader of the county Democrats. The Republican county chairman was his brother, Dr. L. E. Steele, who owned a taxi-and-bus line in Logan. Everybody knew that George and "Doc Noyes" hated each other, and they fought all the time. Those two had even drawn guns on each other in downtown Logan; they had to be pulled off the fight.

I was home one evening before the election when I got a telephone call from George.

"I want you to go over to Logan Storage and get the Studebaker out," he said. "Meet me at eleven o'clock, up at my house. When you come over the rise, just blink your lights once."

I went over and got that Studebaker—a great big car it was—and did what George told me. He slipped out of his place, jumped into the back of that car, and said, "Go on! Go! Go!"

"... Drive up to the East End and turn around!" he said. "Down by the river ... across to the old factory...."

"Where are we going?" I asked.

"You just drive till I tell you to stop!" he snapped. "You got a gun with you?"

I did. I always carried those two little pocket pistols he'd given me. I'd have used them too, if George had said to; but his standing order was, "Never pull them out unless you have to," so I hardly ever used them. (It's harder to get a young man to behave that way these days!)

We crossed a bridge and started up Peck's Mill, when George said, "Pull off here."

I pulled over, and we got out of the car. We waited. We waited there for some time. Finally, George spoke up.

"I don't believe the son-of-a-bitch is gonna show," he said.

Just about then, another car came along, a Hupmobile, one of the biggest cars made in those days.

"That's him. That's him!" said George. "Come on! But be careful. This might be a setup!"

We walked over to the car, and I kept my hands on those two guns in my pockets. In the front of that car was a big black chauffeur, a bodyguard. In the back was George's brother, Doc Noyes.

"'Zat yew, Raymung?" Doc asked. He had a nasally voice, a speech impediment that made him talk through his nose all the time. But he knew who I was.

"Yeah, it's me," I said.

I kept thinking that these two brothers were gonna kill each other. But Doc was still talking to me.

"Yew git in the caw wit' this feller," he said. "If he gits out, you jus' kill the sung-of-a-biktch."

1936: FIRST ELECTION

Doc had said this, but I knew his man would have killed me too if I'd tried anything. Actually, those brothers had put us two to guarding each other, so we wouldn't know what-all was going on between them.

I got into Doc's car, and Doc got into George's Studebaker. That other guard and I talked for a while and, once or twice, we asked ourselves what the hell those men were up to. We decided to get out a couple of times to check on them, and we could see that the Steeles were getting along just fine. They weren't fighting at all. They were working.

My sense was that George was giving Doc the names of Republicans he wanted to see as precinct captains—so-and-so here, and so-and-so over there—and I believe Doc was negotiating too: Why don't you put your weak fellow over there and this good one here?

There were more than a hundred precincts in Logan County back then, and the precinct captains were real important to an election. The captains hired all the campaign workers and determined the amount of money they needed to pay people in order "win" their boss's candidates.

These captains hired the best people they could find, most of them with political jobs and people who got along real well in their neighborhoods. They wanted people who knew the most about politics or those who had the biggest families. The captains worked all through election day, coordinating cars and workers and generally managing the money the party had raised. In some cases, the captains were the ones who paid for votes.

Now most southern West Virginia voters took pride in voting for its own sake, while others took pride in what they were going to get for it—money, a job, a pint of whiskey, or some favor from a politician. Everyone had a good reason to get to the polls on election day, though, and most of the competition for votes was right there at the precincts—among those party captains. They did anything and everything they could to get the votes in for their people. At times, things could get pretty rough around the polling places.

Aside from their election day work, the precinct captains also advised the party leaders on naming election officers in their precincts, or "houses," as we called them. The election officers didn't work outside the "houses"—they were *inside*. The election officers included a poll clerk, who found the voters' names when they came in, and other election commissioners who watched over the whole thing. The election commissioners also "helped" people vote whenever they needed it—and sometimes when they didn't. Some voters couldn't read the names on the ballot. Others might have only one or two candidates they wanted to vote for and they'd call their friend, the commissioner, over to come "help" them. That's what the commissioners did. They helped people vote.

If someone was selling his vote, one of the commissioners would take him over to a table and he'd watch that voter fill out his ballot. Or the voter might just let the commissioner do it for him. (Some of those fellows could vote a ticket faster than a chicken pickin' up corn!) When that voter came out of the building, a commissioner in the doorway gave a sign, which changed every hour or so. That commissioner might tug on his nose or scratch his ear or something to show his faction's people outside that the voter had done what they wanted. Then the precinct captain signed off to somebody else, who met that voter and paid him off.

This is why the choosing of precinct captains and the election officers was so important. A politician's right to name these people working at the polls on election day—at a hundred precincts around the county—gave him a whole lot of political power. For the Democrats in 1936, that power largely belonged to George Steele; for the Republicans, it was his brother, Doc Noyes.

1936: FIRST ELECTION

In the primaries, you might have the clerks and commissioners from the two parties friendly and getting along with each other. Republican clerks and commissioners could do the same things with their voters that Democrats did. Everybody just made sure that the Democratic commissioners helped the Democratic voters while the Republicans did the same for theirs. Any fighting during the primaries, then, would have been between party factions.

During the general, Democrats and Republicans should have been competing for everybody's vote, but sometimes the Democratic leaders made deals with the Republican chairmen. The Republicans might know that they couldn't "win" all their candidates, but they needed to win some of them to make things look good to their people and stay in control. This, I think, was what Doc Noyes and George Steele were arranging in George's Studebaker that night.

I think those two were matching up the captains in the various precincts so that George's people would win—but not by so much as to get Doc Noyes in trouble with his people. Everybody thought Doc Noyes was a Republican feuding with his Democratic brother, but those two were just as tight as brothers could be. Doc Noyes was a Democrat who had fooled us all.

Two or three days later, George and I were walking around town together when he let me in on another little secret.

"Doc and I are gonna meet later in front of Don Chafin's drugstore," he said. "Me and him are gonna fight, and I want you to stop it."

George told me to make sure Butch had some reason to be at the hotel when it happened.

"He ain't as smart as you are. He might knock the hell out of somebody."

Pretty soon, just like George said, we saw Doc Noyes on the other side of Stratton Street and those two started going at it, right across the traffic.

"Goddamn you, Doc!" said George. "I'll knock your damned head off!"

Doc Noyes acted like he was pulling something from his pocket, and that's where I stepped up.

"Don't you pull that gun, Doc!" I shouted.

George stomped across the street—right in front of a car, making it skid real loud—and everybody looked, hoping to see something happen. The Steeles started pushing each other around, acting like they were about to start throwing punches. I got in there between them and pushed both of them back.

"You boys ought to be ashamed of yourselves!" I hollered. "Being brothers and all, behavin' this way!"

Then Doc started in again: "He bee' tawkin' 'bout me. I'm tarrd uv him tawkin' 'bout me! . . . My poh' motha' sai' she ought notta owned him!"

A couple of city policemen ran up to help keep those Steeles apart. I was pushing George back and shouting over my shoulder, "You just go on down the street there, Doc! Get on, now!"

"Boy, ain't that a sight?" one officer told me, shaking his head. "Them bein' brothers and politicians, fighting each other out in the middle of the street like that."

But it was all a big show. Good acting is all it was. Those two politicians had already fixed up the election just the way they wanted.

Election day came along and all the polling places were thick with Democrats and Republicans, out working the polls and battling away. Butch and I guarded Everett Workman the whole day long and didn't hardly have a chance to vote. That evening, when it was all over, we went with Everett into the Aracoma Hotel. Everett was standing there in the lobby, talking to me, and then he turned to Butch.

"You can go on home now," he said. "Come around tomorrow and I'll settle up with you."

1936: FIRST ELECTION

Butch started off, and I turned away for just a moment to say good-bye to him. When I turned back, Everett had disappeared. He was gone; just like that. I looked all around that hotel lobby for him, but Everett was nowhere in sight. "Goddamn, I'm really in for it now."

I was sure someone had kidnapped him. I figured they'd taken him off somewhere to shoot him or something. I took off down the street to find George Steele, and I ran into him coming up the other way.

"I've lost Everett," I said.

"*What?*" said George. "How'd you lose him?"

I told him what had happened on our way back to the Aracoma. We didn't find Everett there, so we went to the Smoke House. George knew the Republicans hadn't taken his candidate—the deal was struck with *them*—but he figured some of those angry miners could have done something to him.

We asked all over the place. Nobody had seen Everett. I went back to the hotel and finally asked a bellhop whether he'd seen the police chief.

"Yeah," he whispered. "He and Mister Ose Richey got on that elevator together! They told me to send you on up."

I knew the Steele brothers were friends, but I didn't know if that meant anything to the candidates. Ose Richey still might have lured Everett upstairs in the Aracoma to whip his ass. I started to take out my pistol, but George stopped me.

"Put that thing back in your pocket!" he said.

"But, damn! Ose might kill Everett!"

"Just put it back in your pocket," George scolded. His voice grew calm.

"Shit, boy, it's all right," he said. "Relax. You've done your job. You're a good man."

We got in the elevator and rode up to the third floor, where we found Everett and Ose Richey. They were sitting together in one of the biggest suites up there. The bar was stocked with all kinds of whiskey, and those two were already on their third or fourth round.

"Come in, boys!" they said. "Come on in!"

"Come on over here, son," Ose Richey said to me. "Goddamn! An hour ago, I would have been scared to see you. I was afraid you might kill me!"

George came up and asked me for my pistols. I handed them over.

"Now, drink all you want to," he said.

I just had a whiskey or two, that was all. But I stayed with those politicians all night long while they partied in that big room up there. They got pretty drunk, and all their people came around—about twenty of the higher-ups, not the precinct workers. At some point, they gave me two fifths of Jack Daniels to carry across the street to Doc Noyes's bus terminal, where he and some of his people were holding a "losing party." I went over there and handed the bottles over to Doc's man, who was sitting out front, guarding the terminal and keeping the peace. It was the big black fellow, the same man I'd sat in the car with that night.

"These are for Doc," I said. "Make sure he gets *both* of them, now!"

He grinned at me before turning and carrying those bottles upstairs.

Later that night, I was sitting with Everett, George Steele, and Ose Richey in the big hotel room. Everett and George were feeling pretty good, of course, because they'd won the election. But Ose was happy, too. He was getting all the beer business. That was the deal. The winners agreed to throw all the customers they could to Ose's beer distributorship. Not too long after the election, Ose's warehouse was a real busy place. The trains were always pulling up on that side-track, where three or four

1936: FIRST ELECTION

men did nothing all day long but load beer on and off the loading dock.

Doc was happy too. He got to run his taxi-bus line and do just about anything he wanted in the county. When a road got rough, a phone call from Doc would fix it. That way, the tires on his buses didn't get all torn up.

So each of these three men—George, Everett, and Ose Richey—was feeling pretty good that night on the third floor of the Aracoma Hotel. I watched Ose lean over to Everett.

"Let's shake hands, Sheriff!" he said.

They shook hands and laughed. Later, Ose turned to Everett Workman again.

"Sheriff," he said, "You think you came out of this deal with the best end of it. But when it's all done and gone, I'll have the best end. I don't have to worry about being sheriff! And when you go out, all I have to do is make me another deal! Yessir, I got the best end of this election!"

Everett smiled. "Well, we'll see about that," he said.

5 Big Bad John

Sherwood: At some point, in a conversation we had before, you said you knew somebody who'd been Sheriff Don Chafin's enforcer. Do you remember that?
Chafin: You mean done his work?... What are you talking about?
Sherwood: I think you said he'd done killings for him.
Chafin: Oh, yeah... John Chafin....

T**HEY CALLED HIM BIG JOHN. HE WAS ONE OF** the best fighters ever in Logan County. He could keep on fighting you, any way you turned him. He wasn't a karate-man, but he could hit you from any way he was—with fists, knees, elbows, you name it.

He was a lot older than I was. But he was strong. He'd exercised in his younger days and always took care of himself.

The first time I remember seeing Big John Chafin was the day I watched him kill a man. It was back in the Hoover days; I was selling newspapers, and my daddy was working at the company store in Omar. I took the paper over to Chauncey, where I had about twenty-five customers, although most of them didn't have any money to pay for it.

Times were real tough there in those days. The upper part of that holler had nothing but a bunch of outlaws living there. They made their whiskey and they bootlegged. They lived in

BIG BAD JOHN

houses built by the Litzen and Smith Coal Company. Litzen and Smith had gone broke during the Depression, and they just abandoned those houses, all of them boarded up and no water or power coming in. The best house went to the meanest fellow. That's the way they played it up there.

Just about anytime I went up Chauncey Holler, I had to fight my way over there and fight my way back, which is probably what made me a pretty good scrapper later on. But Poppy always warned me to stay away from the Chauncey water tank.

All the coal trains stopped at Chauncey to take on water. They stopped at the huge water tank, kept filled from a holding pond right nearby. The railroad had a fellow at that station maintaining a gas pump that pulled the water from the pond to the tank. Every day, in the shade of that tank, there was a group of fellows from around Chauncey who liked to sit and play poker.

All day long, the trains came through to take on water. The railroad man just kept that pump going. And, all day long, those fellows played their penny-ante poker, every one of them unemployed. As the day wore on, they moved around the tank, just following the shade, playing poker.

From where we lived, a shortcut ran right into Chauncey Holler. I could deliver my papers and get home faster by using that shortcut, but I never told my parents about it because it took me right past that water tank, and my father had warned me about that.

One day, when I was about nine or ten years old, I came up there to watch those poker players, laying out their cards and pennies. There, right in the thick of that game, sat Big John Chafin—bigger and meaner than anyone sitting there. Just about the time I got there, a black man walked up, wanting to play cards with them.

"Hey, boys," he said, "How about me dealin' me in?"

John looked up at that fellow, and he recognized him. Right off, John was angry at that man—just for asking to be in the game!

"Now I done told you the other night," Big John said, "that I didn't want to kill you! I caught you stealin' that ace and I told you, 'Don't you never try to get into another game with me!' I told you I'd kill you if you ever tried!"

"Aw, you're just a big ol' bluffer!" the other fellow said. "We're up here in the holler now—and you don't have that big gun on you, no way!"

John raised up and pulled a pistol from under his bib overalls, and he shot that fellow three or four times—just like that. The other man fell back and rolled off the railroad ties. Then he picked himself up and ran over the bank, right into the holding pond, falling facedown into the water, like a big bullfrog. He floated there in the pond, and I knew right then that he was dead.

Goddamn, I just took off running. I ran all the way home and fell right into our front door.

"What's wrong?" my mother asked.

"I just seen some big feller shoot a man, over in Chauncey!"

"You get in here, and you shut up!" she told me. "Don't you say nothing more about it!"

About dark, Carlos Hatfield came knocking at our door, looking for my dad. Carlos had a garage right across the creek from the water tank, and he'd seen the man's body floating in the pond. The company store sold caskets for everybody, and Carlos had come to my father to get one. They got the undertaker, took the man out of the pond, and buried him the next day.

I never heard another word about it. Nobody ever knew exactly who the dead man was—maybe a migrant or somebody.

BIG BAD JOHN

Nobody claimed him. Nobody had even come to see about him, not even the police. I figure Big John and all them had just taken off and left that fellow lying there in the water.

Years later, when I was working on the state road, I met Big John again. I was twenty or twenty-one years old by then, and he had come onto our job site. He was still a great big fellow.

"You know that man?" somebody said. "That's Big, Bad John Chafin."

I didn't know him. I didn't recognize him from the shooting in Chauncey until much, much later. On the job site, they told me that Big John had been working around Mill Creek. He'd been helping someone haul logs on a rail truck, one of those log trucks that ran on wooden rails. He was stout enough a man to roll those logs on and off that truck just using a cane hook. He was big enough to push that truck up those hills himself—at least the smaller ones. He worked just like a mule against those logs.

Mill Creek was a real rough part of Logan County back then. The outlaws down there would get drunk and fight all day. They didn't need a reason; they'd fight just to be fighting. All that knocking around pretty much kept any good folks out of Mill Creek, and Big John Chafin was the meanest of any of them. He could run over anyone down there; he could whip them all.

As tough a place as it was, Mill Creek was still important to the politicians. The people in that precinct could run their liquor any way they wanted; and if they didn't like you, you didn't get their help on anything. In 1936, the politicians decided they'd hire Big John on the roads. They wanted to see whether they could get John to deliver Mill Creek for them on election day.

The state roads had Big John driving a great big old Indiana motor truck. As big as he was, he could pick up almost anything and lift it onto the bed of that trailer by himself—and he was about forty-five years old! But sometimes John had to transport bigger pieces of equipment—caterpillars and dozers and such—and they needed someone to go with him to run those machines up onto his trailer. I knew something about the equipment, so I was picked to go around with Big John.

The first time I rode with him, John just looked at me and scowled.

"So . . . your name's Chafin!" he sneered.

"Yeah."

"Well . . . are you *mean?*"

He was always looking to prove himself, sizing you up to see if you were as big and bad a man as he was.

"No," I said.

"By God, you'd better be!" he warned. "Somebody's gonna beat the shit out of you one of these days!"

"I've always been able to handle myself," I told him, and he looked right at me, as if to say, "Yeah, buddy; I'd really like to try you out. . . ."

We unloaded the truck somewhere and came to a liquor store, where Big John stopped. In those days, J. W. corn whiskey was ninety-eight cents a pint and one-hundred proof. John turned to me.

"You ain't got a dollar on you, do ye?" he asked.

"Yeah."

"Loan me that dollar," he said. "I don't get a payday for another month yet."

I pulled a bill from my pocket, but it was a ten-dollar bill, not a one, and John saw it.

"Loan me that ten," he said. "And I'll give it back to you when I get paid."

So I loaned him ten dollars, and he bought a bottle or two of J. W. corn. He took several drinks and gave me one, and we got along all right that day. Later, when payday rolled around, Big John handed over the ten dollars he owed me. He paid it right back, just like he said he would.

John and I got to working more together. I got to liking him pretty well, and people knew it. At the same time, I was just getting more involved with George Steele and that 1936 election. One day, George came up to see me.

"Raymond," he said, "Have you gotten to know Big John Chafin?"

"Yeah."

"What kind of a feller is he?"

"I believe he's all right."

"I figure he's probably with that other bunch, don't you?" George asked.

He meant the other faction—Don Chafin's. I didn't know whether they were related, but Big John had worked for Don in the past. I figured they'd still be together, and everybody else did too.

"But nobody's ever really talked to him," George said. "Nobody really knows."

Damn right, nobody had talked with Big John. Everybody knew he'd just as soon knock you down as talk to you. Everyone was *afraid* to talk to him, so nobody knew exactly where he stood. But John and I had worked together for some time by then, so I figured I knew him pretty well.

"Hell, I'll talk to him," I said, which pleased George real well.

"John," I said, the next time we got together. "You like your job here, don't you?"

"Oh, yeah," he said. "It's a helluva lot better than haulin' logs. . . . Gettin' more money for it, too!"

"You know who hired you, don't you?"

"I heard that George Steele got me hired," he said.

I got down to the nuts and bolts, just like George taught me.

"John, people are wondering what you're gonna do in this election," I told him. He knew exactly what I meant.

"I've always been loyal to the man who hired me," he said.

"You can't go against Don Chafin, can you?"

"Hell, yeah! His man can't win, and George Steele got me this job. By God, I'm for George Steele!"

Well, that just tickled the hell out of me. I saw George again that evening and told him Big John Chafin stood right there with him. This meant that much of Mill Creek would likely go for him too.

"How do you know that?" George asked.

"I talked to John," I said. "He told me."

George ended up making John his precinct captain over there in Mill Creek. His candidates won that precinct two to one.

After that, John and I became real good friends, and he told me stories of the time when he worked for Don Chafin, when Don was sheriff. He liked to tell me about the big fight he'd had in Logan, right in town there.

Don Chafin hired John as a deputy, even though he wasn't the most steady man around. John was one of these fellows who'd get drunk and stay drunk for a week or two. Whenever he did that, Don fired him as a deputy—and as a mine guard. But he always sent back up for him when he needed something done.

It must have been in the early twenties when Don Chafin was working to keep the union out of here. John liked to drink and, I'm telling you, he really got drunk. He'd get himself fired and then wait for a time when Don needed him again. That's what happened when the sheriff heard about this big union man coming in from Ohio.

"John," he said. "Are you sober?"

"Yeah."

"I've got a job for you."

"Am I back on the payroll?"

"Yeah, you're on the payroll.... I've got a man coming in here on a train this evening. I want you to go over to the mercantile and get yourself the best suit you can find. I want you to put it on; I want you to look as good as a coal operator. And when that man gets off the train, I want you to whup him. Now, John, I'm telling you, he's mean."

"Do you think I can whup him?"

Don Chafin didn't bat an eye, he just looked right at Big John.

"By God, you'd better," he said. "Otherwise, you're likely to go the way some of the rest of them have gone around here."

John figured that meant he'd get tossed into the powerhouse. He told me a lot of miners who wouldn't work—men who were "causing trouble" or organizing the union—were taken over to the powerhouse and thrown into the furnace there. People around here still wonder about that, but John told me it was true.

So the sheriff sent John over to the Logan Mercantile to get himself a suit. John bought it all—a coat and hat and a new pair of shoes—and he had everything on him that evening when he went to meet that union man from Ohio.

Just before the train came in, John made a deal with a taxi driver—a man named Reed—to be watching for that union organizer. Reed was another mean one, and he was nervy too. He knew not to ask any questions, not to mess with whatever Big John Chafin was up to.

When the Ohio man came off that train, he started looking around for a taxi. There was Reed, all ready for him. That man started to get into his taxi when Big John came up.

"Hey, buddy," he said. "That's my taxi."

"No, sir," the other said. "This taxi is mine!"

Nobody knew what was going to happen when John started into it with this fellow, because John always carried a gun. But, goddamn, they went at it. Reed and some others had to push that taxi out of the way just to give them room to fight.

By and by, John started getting the best of the other fellow, and that organizer slipped away from him. He jumped into another cab—one with a driver who wasn't as mean as Reed—and they drove downtown to find a justice of the peace. That union man planned on getting a warrant against Big John.

But John figured on that and took off running. He went around the railroad station, took a shortcut, and beat that taxi to the J.P.'s office. When the man's cab pulled up, John was waiting there to give him another round. By God, they went into it again, right out in front of the county courthouse!

Eventually, the police came over and arrested them both on the street. Don Chafin—who controlled just about everything in Logan, including the police and the J.P.—walked up to them.

"What's going on here, boys?" he said. "John, what's the matter with you? You fighting again?"

"These goddamned union son-of-a-bitches ain't coming in here and takin' over!" said John.

"Now, John, I've told you about starting trouble down here," the sheriff said. "You've already killed four or five people, and here you are beating up on this fellow. I believe we're gonna have to put you in jail this time."

Then the sheriff turned to the union organizer. "What about you, buddy? Where are you from?"

By this time, John had beaten this fellow all to hell and back, and he'd seen all of Logan County that he wanted.

"I'm from Ohio," he said.

"Well, I figure a year or so in jail will do you both some good," said Don. "Go on, squire, take 'em on down there!"

BIG BAD JOHN 69

"Wait a minute!" said the Ohio man. "If you people just let me catch a train out of here, you'll never see me again."

"What about you, John?" the sheriff said. "If I let you go, are you gonna quit all this fighting?"

"Yeah, I won't do it no more."

So Don's men got that fellow's suitcase and put him back on the train. He left Logan County and no one ever heard anything more about him after that.

Poor old John worked on the state road for years and years. Finally, he grew old. He'd fought in World War I, so he was getting some veterans' pension money and Social Security.

I was downtown one day, around 1950, when I ran into Big John, and we talked.

"Raymond," he said. "I need a place to stay. You have that little farm of yours. I'll pay you if you let me stay with you. I could help with the garden and everything."

The place he was talking about was a small farm on Cow Creek where I raised a garden and some hogs, chickens, and a couple of cows. The place needed a fair amount of work to keep it up, so I told John I'd ask Louise about it.

We ended up building an extra room, and John came to stay with us. He made his home there, doing some work, and cooking for us all. John was a real good cook; he made cornbread and stuff like that. He was clean as a pin, too.

He kept bees and a cow that he'd bought himself. He milked that cow—mine, too—and he put the milk into a butter churn we had. Almost every day you could see Big Bad John sitting there churning butter. He sold butter and milk to the neighbors, or he'd just give it away.

Once in a while, John and I would go down to the market together, and he'd pick us out a big beef steer. We'd take the steer home on the truck, slaughter it, and put it in the deep-freeze.

Big John was smart, politically, having worked for Don Chafin. He knew how to work an election, how to talk to people. I used him politically, but I never did have him fighting or whipping anyone. I didn't run my campaigns like that. If I couldn't talk a person into doing a thing, or convince them of it somehow, I just let them go. I'm the same way yet. I'll offer work, and I'll pay people to do it; but if they don't want to do it, I don't push it. Won't ask them again, either.

I did see John in one bad fight—I'd say around 1951, when our daughter Margaret was about two years old. I was there, in this beer joint, when it started. I came in with a friend of mine, and Big John was just sitting in there, about half drunk.

"What you say there, Stud?" I called out to him. (Not everybody could talk to Big John like that, but he was still living with us. I could say just about anything I wanted to him.)

" 'Ello!" he said. "Come on, sit down, boys! I'll buy you a drink!"

"No thanks, buddy, we're just gettin' a pint for ourselves!"

Just then, two women walked into the place.

"Hey, John, honey!" they said. These two had been "monkeys," I think, but they'd gotten too old to monkey around. John was pretty old himself, but he knew those two, so he called them over to join him.

"Sit down, girls!" he said. "I'll buy you a beer!"

They sat down with him, and just about that time here come these two other fellows. I guess they'd been with these women, because they were acting a little bit put off that they were sitting with Big John.

"What are you doin' over there?" said one. He was a miner named Ira White, and he came from a real tough family. His father was a man named "Mean Will" White, a man so mean that somebody'd shot his eye out.

"John's gonna buy us a beer," the women told Ira and his friend.

BIG BAD JOHN

"By God, we'll buy your beer!"

I saw John looking up at Ira White, and I wondered whether he still carried that pistol on him.

"All right," John said to Ira. "You just treat these women lady-like. I'm just buying them a beer, and it don't mean a damned thing. So, you just treat them with respect!"

"I'll give you some respect!" said Ira, rearing up.

John just jumped right out of that chair and hit him one time. Ira White went clean over, right into the heating stove. He took the whole thing down with him as he fell, and soon one whole end of that bar was filled with ashes and smoke.

But that didn't stop those two. John and Ira White went at it, fighting all over that place. Two or three of the others started getting up to pull them apart, but I figured on letting them play it out. When the others stood up to stop it, I stood up, too, and pointed straight at them.

"Sit down, boys!" I hollered. "Don't you dare rise up! Goddamn, just let 'em fight! By God, you sit down!"

Those fellows knew me, and I was still a big man myself back then, so they just fell back into their seats. Then John got to beating Ira pretty bad, so I went over and shook him.

"All right, John, let him up!" I said.

Ira White got out from under John and just took off out of that place, leaving his hat and glasses behind. John was brushing himself off, grumbling—kind of put off that I'd stopped the fight so soon.

"Now that son-of-a-bitch is gonna want to try me again," he said.

He couldn't have been more wrong about that. Two or three days later, I was at my place when I heard somebody yelling for me outside. I came down, and Ira White was standing there.

"Hey, Raymond!" he said. "I just wanted to thank you for pulling Big John Chafin off me the other night. He might have killed me if it hadn't been for you!"

Ira had been hurt pretty bad—so bad, he'd taken a couple days off work to heal up—but he was glad to be alive.

"You know," he said, "I didn't realize who I was getting into it with!"

"I thought you figured John was too old to fight you," I told him. "By God, he sure turned it around on you."

"He sure as hell did," Ira admitted. "I'll never tangle with him again. And I brought it all on myself. . . . Will you go apologize to him for me, Raymond?"

I said I would, and I did. After that, John and Ira White got to talking, and they got to be all right together. Sometime afterward, John told me he'd always wanted to try Ira in a fight because Ira was so damned mean. Fighting was really like a sport to those men.

But John was also the best-hearted fellow you've ever seen, almost like a father to me. As he got older, he grew to like people—just about everybody—and everybody liked him. To Louise and me, Big John Chafin was as nice a man as he could be. He was crazy about our daughter, Margaret, who was just a little girl at that time. He worshipped her more than anything, and he just about raised her.

Still, there were times when he'd get drunk, and when that happened, John got sad. He got just miserable, crying about "those men"—all the men he'd killed. I asked him once how many there'd been. He didn't even know.

It got on Louise's nerves whenever John started crying. He realized this, so he came to us one day and told us he'd be moving out. He'd stayed at our place about three or four years by then.

So John moved out, rented himself a little shanty near Barnabus, and he lived there for a while. Every so often, he'd come back up to spend some time with us, have a meal and stay a night or two. By this time, he was getting up in years—well into his seventies.

Then, in 1958, Big John Chafin had a stroke. He had some family, but they never did bother with him much, so Louise would fix him something to eat, and I would take it up to his place at Barnabus. But John never did get any better, so I checked him into the VA hospital in Huntington.

I drove there to see him about once a week. I took him cigarettes and candy or some dish that Louise had fixed. We talked together in his room for an hour or two, and then I went home. I believe I was the only one who ever did that, taking him things and all.

John told me he wanted to be buried in a fancy, tailor-made suit that he'd bought for himself. He said he paid one-hundred and twenty-five dollars for that suit and hadn't worn it but once or twice. He had a big, white Stetson hat that he liked. Boy, he really loved to wear those Stetsons. There was no mistaking Big John Chafin when you saw that hat coming down the street.

But John didn't look so good the last time I visited him. I knew he was in bad shape because they'd given him his own room.

"John, you feeling worse?"

"Yeah, I ain't feeling so good, Raymond."

"Is there anything you want me to do for you?" I asked him.

"Raymond," he said, "can you get forgiveness for killing people?"

"I don't know, John. They tell me you can. They tell me it's in the Bible, but I ain't never read the Bible. . . . They say you can get forgiveness for anything, if you pray hard enough."

"Do you think I'm gonna die?"

"You're in pretty bad shape," I said. "You want to talk about it?"

"No," he said. "When you've killed people . . . well, I just wondered if you can get forgiveness."

A day or two after that, somebody called and told us that

John had passed away. His brother came in to make the funeral arrangements. I told him about the suit John wanted to be buried in, but the family had him dressed in something else instead.

It was a big funeral. The Church of Christ was full, running over with people. They buried Big John in the Curry cemetery, right here on Cow Creek.

6 Politics

PEOPLE TODAY REALLY DON'T KNOW ANY-thing about politics; they have no idea of what it's all about. You think you pick a man for governor. I think I pick one. Another man thinks he picks one. But we don't pick them. I don't care to get into it right now, but I know. I've seen how it's done. In 1936, it operated just the way I've described, and it *still* operates that way—in Logan, or Charleston or, I think, just about anywhere. People are just smarter with it now.

Ose Richey got to run his beer business, Everett Workman got the sheriff's office, and Doc Steele got to run his buses on good roads. George Steele was likely taking his part of the deal from everyone. I'm sure somebody took care of him. But they all won. I won. At the time, I thought it was a pretty good way of doing things. I'd watched George Steele operate, and that gave me a good sense of how to handle things when I got ready to run my own campaigns.

After the '36 election, I went back to my job on the state road. I worked real hard, making my way up to truck driver. I was still keeping my dad and mother, and the new job had taken us off the WPA.

My association with George Steele and his people quickly allowed me to start getting some things done for Cow Creek, and one of the first things I did was get a school in there. I got that school mostly for my Uncle Harley Curry, the third child of Grandma Mary and Grandpa Tommy Curry.[1]

Harley was kind of a go-getter—a ladies' man. He fooled around and fooled around and the next thing you know, he was married to Ethel White. (Ethel's daddy was "Mean Will" White, the man so mean that someone shot his eye out.) Ethel had been a widow with five children. But after Uncle Harley married her, they had ten or eleven of their own, making fifteen or sixteen all together.

Harley stayed away from home a lot, but he worked in the mines and in U. G. Browning's store. He had a pretty good education; he could work a cash register and he ran a service station before the Depression. Around 1929, Harley was working on a car or a truck at that station when another car backed over him and crushed him through his chest. That messed him up pretty good. It was several years before he could work again, but he recovered.

Everybody liked Uncle Harley. He wasn't a big man, but he had good foresight and he was a good planner. He liked to hunker down when he talked to you. No matter where you met him—on the street or anywhere—Uncle Harley would just squat down and start rolling himself a cigarette. You'd find yourself squatting down there with him while Harley rolled his paper full of Prince Albert. He was also an A-number-one farmer, and he read a lot—even with all those kids around. I never knew one of those children ever to be in trouble, either.

---

1. This Harley Curry is not related to the man with the taxi-bus line in chapter 2.—T. S.

So one of the first things I did was get a school for Harley's kids. That school was good for Harley and other folks around here, but it turned out to be a good thing for me, too, because it brought my wife, Louise, to Cow Creek. Louise's mother had married Julius Dingess after Art Chambers died. Julius worked as a blacksmith, and he helped send Louise to college. She went to Concord and then to Morris Harvey, where she got her teaching degree.[2]

When Louise came back to Logan County, she became the teacher at the school and boarded with Uncle Harley and his family. I went up to see him from time to time and I met her that way. A couple of weeks after we met, Louise and I were going out in my new pickup truck. Three or four weeks after that, we were married.

One of the reasons I married Louise is because she was so smart. I wanted somebody who was better educated than I was. She did a lot of reading—still does—and she's always been with me politically. (Her mother had told her to pick herself out a good Democrat, and I guess I measured up.)

Louise and I lived in Barnabus and she taught at the head of Cow Creek, still boarding with Uncle Harley during the week. Harley often rode his horse to our place and stayed there all night. After getting the school, we talked about all kinds of other things we could get for Cow Creek. At the time, I was just getting started in politics, and Harley encouraged me to stick with it.

"You stay right in there, Raymond," he said. "One of these days you might get up to where we can get a road on Cow Creek. You tell me who you want to elect and I'll help you elect them, and we'll get us a road up here!"

We had something of a road on the lower end of the creek—the old WPA road ran from the Left Fork to Barnabus. But it

---

2. The college has since been renamed the University of Charleston.—T. S.

was just an old dirt road then, hardly wide enough for people with wagons to back up and turn around. They were having the hardest time in the world on it.

Harley and I swore that we'd put a good road all the way up the creek, clear to the top of the mountain, if we ever got the chance. We sat in my place of an evening and planned the whole thing out: "We'll run a bridge across the creek over here, and run the road across the hill over there," and so on. We'd both walked that way so many times we knew practically every rock and turn in it.

During the day I drove a truck for the state road commission. The state roads were divided into sections, and ours ran from Logan to the Mount View Inn. There'd be four or five of us working on it during the summertime but, in winter, it was usually just me and one other fellow, the foreman.

Once in a while the state sent us a new piece of equipment, a tractor or a grader or something. Then they just left it sitting there on our job site while they hunted up somebody who knew how to operate it. I figured it wasn't any good having that big machine just sitting there, so I jumped into it and taught myself how it worked. I'd drive it around on the site and work the controls until I could operate anything they sent up there. Nobody else on the crew ever said anything about it, probably because they knew I was still "George Steele's boy."

I guess you could say this was an advantage for me, and you'd be right. Buddy, I took every advantage I could get. If you don't try to get ahead in life, you're never going to do anything. I don't care who you are. I never did anybody wrong. I never knocked anybody off a job, and I never crooked anyone. But I took any advantage I had. Remember, I never had more than a seventh-grade education, and that was it. So I learned wherever I could and took what advantages there were. Eventually, a road foreman's job came open on our section, and I got it.

POLITICS

At the same time, I was still helping people where I could. If somebody needed something, I knew where to go—to the sheriff, George Steele, or whoever. Politically, I became a precinct captain at Barnabus, hiring people to work the precinct during elections and organizing campaign meetings in the towns all around here.

The campaign meetings were important. People up Cow Creek always had a tough time of getting in and out. Nobody had television then; nobody had a radio. We didn't even get electricity up here until 1945. News was passed the way it always had been; people visited with each other and, at election time, we held meetings.

I figured out what I was doing pretty fast as a precinct captain—how to speak well, how to introduce people, and how to tell people what they wanted to hear. For the 1938 election, I became the speaker at these meetings all around here, from Logan to the head of Island Creek.

We had meetings at all the schoolhouses, up and down the creek—in Stirrat, Barnabus, Omar, Pine Creek, Chauncey and Micco. We started at Stirrat, say, at six o'clock. People from the neighborhood came in and I got there at 6:15 to talk for maybe fifteen minutes. That's all I needed. If the crowd was small, and I didn't want to use up all my time, I'd cut it short. I told people what we wanted the politicians to do for us—to improve this school or build that road. I built up the crowd, and then I turned things over to the chairman, usually a precinct captain. The chairman got up there and said whatever he had to say. Then he introduced the candidates, and generally kept things rolling. By then, though, I'd be long gone.

It was kind of like riding the Pony Express. I always had a man outside, waiting in a car with the motor running. As soon as I was done at one place, I hopped into that car and we raced to the next stop, then to the next, and then another after that. On my way out, if anybody tried to holler at me or ask me something, I just told them I had another meeting and kept going. I didn't have time to fool with people; I jumped into that car and went. Sometimes I'd pick up a candidate who'd just spoken and I'd take him with me to the next meeting, but I ran a tight schedule, buddy.

The candidates all did the same thing. While I was talking at Omar, one of them might be talking in Micco, or Chauncey, or some other place, giving me time to get there. A candidate might speak before me in one place and after me in another. But whenever I came in, whoever was talking knew that his time was up. That man knew to sit down, or he didn't get our support. The candidates told people what they planned to do; I told them what I'd make *sure* the candidates did once we elected them. We talked to people all over this county that way.

The other factions could never get their meetings together like that. If one of their people wanted to talk at our meetings, that was fine—as long as ours were done first. But when *our* side was done talking, most people were done listening. Those other groups could never get the support we had on this creek.

The politicians don't do meetings like that anymore. That's why we have such idiots in politics today. You don't get good candidates, and there's no one with enough influence to hold them to their promises. Back then, we put good people into office and we made sure they did everything they'd said they were going to do.

By 1940, most people knew Raymond Chafin. They came to me for things. Our election-meeting posters read, "Raymond Chafin. Be Here at 7:30 p.m." But George Steele was the man most responsible for our success in those days. He was a manager, and a good one. Among other things, George knew how to throw the opposition off.

If I wanted to kill you off politically, for example, I'd go to one of your very best friends and say, "You know, if your man would only do such-and-so, it would make him popular as hell with those people...." Maybe I'd say, "Those Currys on Cow Creek ain't for your man no way. He ought to get out there and start telling everybody about those Currys."

Before you know it, that candidate is somewhere up Cow Creek, taking a stand: "People, you know how them Currys are; you oughta get rid of them on this creek!" What he doesn't know is that the Currys are married into damn-near *everybody* up there. People might not like some of them, but they sure don't want you talking about their own! That candidate's ship is sunk—and he's done it to himself!

But one of the best political tricks I've ever seen was a game that one of my own people turned around on me.

George Steele and I were working together one primary and we had everything organized pretty well. We got to choosing our precinct captains and we decided to leave out a cousin of mine, a man who had helped George several times up in Pine Creek. He was a coal miner named Kess Curry.

Now Cousin Kess was about as smart as any man could be, and he was a real good precinct captain—when he was sober, that is. But Kess had a drinking problem. He'd gotten to where we couldn't depend on him for election day, so we had to quit Kess and get another man as Pine Creek's precinct captain. Of course, that didn't go down too well with old Kess and he came to talk to me about it.

"Raymond," he said, "George don't want me to be captain this year!"

"That's right, Kess," I told him. "I'll be honest with you.

You've been drinking too much, and we can't let you run things like that."

Still, I felt bad about cutting him out of everything, so I told Kess I'd get him back in if he helped us out on Pine Creek and did it right.

I didn't know it, but Kess was really angry with us, and he was a smart man, politically. Pine Creek had actually been sewn-up in our favor, and we knew it. But Kess figured on a way of undoing everything there and getting even with us.

A prostitute lived in that precinct, a woman who drank with half the men on Pine Creek, and "laid in the sand-house" with the rest. The women up there knew her as a no-account monkey—always monkeying around with their men—and they wanted nothing to do with her. Kess went to have a talk with that woman.

"I want you to help us with the election," he told her. "I'll pay you ten dollars to put one of these cards on every house.... Don't give 'em to the men, though. We want the women to vote this time around. Make sure and give these cards to the *wives.*"

The cards, of course, were our slates—all our candidates' names were printed on them. So Kess stood back and watched that woman do what he'd asked. When she was done, Kess gave her ten dollars in coal-company scrip, drawn from the company office.

After that, of course, it was even-Steven between Kess and us. On election night, I went into the precinct office and saw the results. Our candidates got *nailed* in Pine Creek, and we'd thought we were solid there.

"What the hell happened?" I asked a clerk.

"You got most of the men, Raymond," he told me, "But every woman up that creek voted against you! They all came in saying the same thing: 'I ain't votin' for nobody that whore is for!'"

We took Kess back after that. The trick was such a good one, I just couldn't get mad at him.

I got to rising through the ranks on the state roads until 1942, when I became county roads superintendent in Logan County. I liked that job a whole lot. But sometime after that, I had a run-in with the state governor, M. M. Neely.

George Steele and M. M. Neely never had gotten along very well. Neely was from the northern part of the state. He was elected in 1940, beating our man, R. Carl Andrews. The fact that we'd worked against him didn't make things look too good for us once Neely became governor.

More specifically, things didn't look too good for me, as high up as I'd gotten on the state roads. I wasn't a politician who did nothing; I'd done a good job as Logan's roads superintendent. I worked hard, people knew it, and I was popular. I liked helping them, and I liked my work, so my influence stayed pretty high in the early forties.

In the meantime, though, Everett Workman had split with George Steele and was trying to push him out of the picture entirely. Everett had gone out as sheriff and become county Democratic chairman, a powerful position. His faction, which had Governor Neely behind it, wanted me to join up. But George would never concede power to them, so I stuck with him. George didn't think Everett had enough influence to get me in trouble with the state roads, so I stayed loyal to him and kept away from Everett's bunch—even after George moved away to a farm in Virginia. The decision to stick with George didn't hurt me, not for some time after the 1940 election.

One morning, in February 1944, I was working out on the road when a bookkeeper called me up. Governor Neely wanted to hear from me, just as quick as I could get to a phone. I came into that office and called the governor in Charleston.

"Raymond," he said, "I need to see you. When can you come over?"

"You're the governor," I said. "Anytime you say."

He asked if I could come to Charleston that same day and I said I would. Then he added something else: "Do you have a fellow named Blutcher Sias working for you?"

"I sure have."

"Bring Blutcher with you," Neely said.

Blutcher Sias, who was crippled and walked with a crutch, was a very honorable man whose wife happened to be on the county Democratic Executive Committee. Mandy Sias held the swing vote on a very important issue. She could say whether the election officers at the polls in 1944 would be George Steele's people or Everett Workman's. It didn't take long to figure why M. M. Neely wanted to see me and Blutcher. The governor, who would be running for U.S. Senate that year, was taking a new interest in Logan County politics.

I found Blutcher and said, "Let's go, buddy. The governor wants to see us."

Blutcher got all excited. He thought, as I did, that our days of being political "outcasts" were over.

"Goddamn! The governor wants to see me?" he said. "My God, Raymond! I believe we're gonna get back in!"

"Yeah, it sure looks that way," I said. "Looks like he wants to line us up."

We drove to Charleston in my state car—drove right up to the capitol building.

"My name's Raymond Chafin," I told the receptionist inside. "The governor wants to see me and Mr. Sias here."

M. M. Neely came to the door of his office and offered his hand, which had clubbed fingers.

"How are you, Raymond?" he asked.

"Just fine, governor," I said, shaking that hand.

"Mr. Sias, isn't it? Yes, Yes. Come on in, gentlemen!"

We sat down and I got right to the point, something that George Steele had taught me.

"What can we do for you, Governor?"

"Well," he said, "I want to see some changes over there in Logan County. And you are the key to it, Raymond; you and Mr. Sias here."

I thought, "Well, that's good enough...."

"There'll be no more George Steele!" Neely declared. "We're getting rid of him and his whole faction!"

Blutcher was sitting next to me, and I could see that he was beginning to tense up. He was already reaching for his crutch. I was a little that way myself, but I wanted to hear more.

"Just what do you mean by that, Governor?" I asked.

"I want you to get away from that bunch and join Everett Workman's faction. To hell with George Steele. I never liked him much, anyway. Now, both of you work for the state roads, and you'll do exactly as I say, or you won't have a job in my administration!"

As mean a man as I was back then, it was all I could do to keep myself in control. I sat there, studying on what the governor had said. Truthfully, I considered jumping across that desk and whipping that man's ass all over his office.

But Governor Neely wasn't a total fool. He must have known he was rubbing us the wrong way, so he tried to build us back up some.

"You know I'll pay you more money," he said. "And you'll do a lot better—you'll go a long ways—if you stay with the state roads."

By that time, though, I'd heard enough.

"Governor," I said, "George Steele was the man who took me off relief. And, goddammit, I don't have to work for you! I don't have to kiss no-goddamn-body's ass! If that what it takes for me to work for you, you can just take your job and ram it up yours!"

"By God," said Blutcher, scrambling up with his crutch, "That goes for me too! You club-fisted son of a bitch!"

I thought Blutcher was going to wallop the governor with that crutch of his, and Governor Neely must have thought the same thing because he hit a button at his desk that called the state policemen in there. Two great-big officers came busting through that door and took hold of me while the governor fired Blutcher and me, right on the spot.

"How'd you men get here?" he asked.

"In a state car," I said.

"Then you can just put the keys on this desk!" he said. "And get back to Logan any way you can."

"I left the keys in the car," I told him.

He ordered us out at that point. The state policemen—one under each arm—practically lifted me off the floor, leading me out of there with Blutcher right behind. Now, I knew one of these officers. He'd been stationed in Logan, and he knew me well. He knew I was a pretty tough customer.

"Lookie here, Raymond," he said, once we were outside. "You don't want no trouble here, and I don't want to have to put you in jail. If we can't handle you, we'll call in six more who will. Why don't you just go on home? We don't care about the damned car. Let 'em hunt for it."

I thought that was pretty nice of that fellow, so I thanked him. On the way back to the car, though, Blutcher came up with another idea.

"Why don't we get the keys out of that car," he said, "and just throw them in the river!"

"Don't have to," I grinned. "I had them in my pocket all along."

"I used to pitch baseball, son," said Blutcher. "Give 'em on over here!"

Let me tell you, even on crutches, Blutcher Sias could wind up and throw pretty good. Those keys sailed into the air, cleared the boulevard and disappeared over the north bank of the Kanawha River. We laughed about it more than once on the bus trip back to Logan.

My dismissal stayed in newspapers for about a week. Nobody knew it then, but the whole incident had served to fire me up. I was hell-bent to beat the tar out of Everett Workman's crew and retake the next election in Logan County. I did it with the help of a man named John Morrison.

John and I had worked together on the state roads and we liked each other. He was a Republican, but he owed George Steele a big favor. John's brother had been in some serious trouble, but John took the rap for him—even going to the state penitentiary. Then George got a state road job for John, which helped get him out of prison. When I was rising up into management, I kept John on the payroll. I always gave him a decent truck to drive—even when the Democrats were giving me hell for it. I didn't care. John was a good fellow, and he was my friend. Also, by the time of my firing, John had gotten high up in the Republican party. I went to him after my little run-in with the governor.

"John," I said. "I need you to help me out here. The Democrats have done kicked my ass."

"What do you want?"

I knew exactly what I wanted. I wanted things the way they'd been for George and Doc Steele for the general election back in 1936.

"I want so-and-so as a precinct captain here," I said. "And so-and-so over there, and that other one over there. . . ."

"By golly," said John, "George Steele helped me out. He got me a job and got me out of prison. I'll be with you, Raymond."

So John helped get all my Republican friends into those positions, just the way I wanted. That didn't make everything easy, though. I still had to work hard for the primary. I took charge of what was left of George Steele's faction. I organized, rallied our people, and set up campaign meetings. It all paid off. When primary day came around and Logan County voted, our candidates beat just about every damned name Everett Workman had sent up against us.

When the dust cleared from that election, most folks who were watching politics knew that Raymond Chafin of Logan County was someone to reckon with.

7 Inroads

JOHN MORRISON HELPED ME IN MORE THAN one way that year. Since leaving the state roads, he'd been running a diner—the Guyan Barbeque. When the word got around that I'd been fired, John told me not to bother buying food anyplace else.

"You and your wife just come in here to eat!" he said. "I won't charge you a dime."

So, Louise and I went to the Guyan Barbeque to eat from time to time, and sometimes I went in there on my own. I'd go in and order myself something from the menu, but John always insisted on cooking me a steak.

One day, I was having lunch in there when John came over to me and pointed out a man sitting in another booth.

"See that fellow?" he said. "That's T. R. Workman, vice president of West Virginia Coal and Coke. If you asked him, he might give you a job."

I told John there was no way I'd get hired there, since I'd been blackballed by all the coal companies. But he went over to talk with the coal executive. Before long, John was introducing me to T. R. Workman.

Now I have to tell you that Ramey Workman was absolutely the worst—the all-time *worst*—Republican that ever walked this county. There hasn't been *anyone* who was a worse Republican than Ramey Workman. He fought the Democrats every which way possible, dirty and clean, but he never could pick a candidate who could win.

"I've read about you," Workman said when I'd sat down. "Those Democrats kicked you around in Charleston, didn't they?"

I had to admit it. They sure had.

"How would you like to come to Omar and work?" he said. "Come on up; I'll give you a job."

"Now, Mr. Workman," I told him, "There ain't no use for me to come up there. I've been blackballed."

"I haven't blackballed you, have I?" he said. "You come up to Omar on Monday morning."

It was hard to turn down. I'd had other offers for construction jobs, but I didn't want to go back to that if I could get away from it. I could do the work; I could operate just about any machine they had. But most of them only paid seventy-five or eighty cents an hour. Mr. Workman's offer was much more generous and well worth thinking about.

John left the table at some point, and I stayed to talk some more with Ramey Workman. Eventually, we came to the biggest question between us.

"If I gave you a job," he said. "What would you do about politics?"

"Well, sir, let's just make things plain," I said. "I need a job more than anything in the world. But politics is going to have to be my own business. You know how I am, Mr. Workman, and I know how you are. You know I've helped to elect a lot of Democrats around here. Why can't each of us do what he has to—and just let the other one be?"

I went on to tell him what he already knew: that there were some real son-of-a-bitches—Democrats—that I wanted to get out of power.

"And I'm gonna get them," I assured him. "But you let me do it my way."

The coal operator nodded, agreeing not to interfere with my politics.

"I'll tell you something else I can do for you," I said. "I may need the job but, really, you need me. Honestly, Mr. Workman, you don't know a damned thing about politics in this county! You know these people would love to get a whack at you if they could. If the police could ever get you in that jailhouse, they'd just tear that place up with you!"

He knew it was true. Anytime the county deputies caught one of his mining officials even a little bit drunk, they'd just toss that man into jail—and they didn't let them alone there, either! Ramey Workman could never just go someplace to have a drink. If he did, he always took his chauffeur. He was smart enough to know that hiring Raymond Chafin couldn't hurt him one bit.

"By God, I like you," he said. "I like the way you talk!"

"Well, there ain't no use in me coming up there to work for you if you just have to fire me in a few days. It wouldn't do me any good—and it sure as hell wouldn't help you, either."

Soon after that, I was working at West Virginia Coal and Coke as a foreman, making twelve dollars and fifty cents a day—top wages even for a section boss in the mines. Nobody working outside had ever made that kind of money.

Truthfully, though, I didn't like it too much. With my state job, I'd gotten used to traveling all over the place. If I needed to go to Charleston for a few hours, I could always go. If I wanted to attend somebody's funeral, I went. But at West Virginia Coal and Coke, I had to stay on that same job all day long, and it nearly killed me. Still, I needed the money—and the money was good.

One day, after I'd been working for West Virginia Coal and Coke for several months, a shovel operator came in drunk, so they fired him. They'd already fired this fellow four or five times before; but now the war was on, and there wasn't anyone around to replace him. They were in a fix. There was a pile of gravel waiting to be loaded at Chauncey. The boss, O. M. Holliday, came to me.

"Do you think you can run that shovel, Raymond?" he asked.

"Well that's an awful little thing," I told him. "I don't know whether I can or not...."

"You operate that shovel and we'll give you top wages—boss's rate, ten hours a day."

"No," I said. "I want to be fair with you. If you're really letting that other fellow go, I just might want his job for good. Let me try it out at my own wage and see how I like it."

The work meant digging up sand and gravel, moving it out to mix into concrete, and grading the roads. I was good at this; it was really my profession, so I liked it real well. I ended up working that shovel for two or three years.

One day, O. M. Holliday came to me and said, "We're doing a lot of grading up at Number Nineteen. We're shutting down four tipples and running the coal to the one at Stirrat. We need you to quit the shovel and help grade the motor road."

The motor road was a roadbed that held four narrow-gauge tracks that ran from the mines to the new tipple. The company had brought some really big equipment for that roadbed, the biggest ever up that hollow. There had never been this big a job up there before, so it had been contracted out to someone else.

I went up to the site and looked things over with Ramey Workman and O. M. Holliday. Right away, I could see that the job foreman didn't know what he was doing.

"They've already started out wrong," I told them. "He hasn't sited the road high enough. By the look of the slope-stakes, it won't go back to where you want it."

Just then, the main contractor—an Italian fellow—drove up in a big white Cadillac. He got out of that car and looked up the hill.

"Hey-hey-hey!" he shouted to his foreman. "You come on down here! Man, you're not far enough up that hill! Get that dozer in there and slope it right!. . ."

When Holliday and Workman saw this, they figured they couldn't go wrong with me. They had me oversee all the work for that motor road, and we did it just the way they wanted.

After that, I went back to my job as a shovel operator for a few months. Then they called me again. The company had enlarged a power-generation plant at Chauncey Holler for the new coal tipple, and they needed more water through there. They wanted me to build a dam. Before it was over, I'd built them *two* dams and they had all the water they needed for that power plant.

During the time I worked on those projects—from 1944 to 1952—I pretty much stayed out of politics. I did do some lobbying and helped elect a candidate or two, but mostly I watched elections from the sidelines. I never got out in the open on anything; you might say I was still learning my way around.

Then, sometime before the '52 election, Ramey Workman came to me and suggested that I go back to working on the state roads. He wasn't the only one. Some of our Democratic politicians had already been coming to me with the same idea.

Everybody was unhappy with the way things had been going—mostly with the people who were in charge of the county roads. Good road service was getting hard to come by, and a lot of things that needed doing weren't getting done. The local politicians wanted me to help them run their campaigns, and the state road supervisor's job would help me do it; the job was a big political office in this county. A bunch of them came to see me at my house, led by a young man named Ray Watts.

Ray was a great Logan County politician. He walked fast, made the right connections, and got along with everybody. Ray was a casual person—not a suit-every-day man—and he'd been real popular with the miners because he'd been a checkweighman. The county checkweighman makes sure the companies' scales stay accurate. Miners were still paid by the ton in those days, so the checkweighman was an important man to them. The United Mine Workers was big on Ray Watts.

When he came to me, Ray had decided to run for county sheriff, which was always an important position in West Virginia. Aside from being the chief law-enforcement officer in the county, the sheriff collects the taxes, giving him a lot of political power. Grover Combs had been sheriff up until then, but he couldn't succeed himself, so Grover and some others were going to help Ray win the primary against Floyd Murphy. I wasn't so sure whether they could win it, though, and I told Ray as much when he and the others came to see me that day.

"I don't know whether we can cut this thing for you or not," I said. "Floyd Murphy's real popular. He's been a justice of the peace and he's treated people real good. You've got a hard way to go, Ray. I doubt if you can win."

But, being good politicians, they talked me into it. I agreed to become roads supervisor again, even though it meant a pay cut for me, working for the state. If Ramey Workman hadn't offered to let me do the occasional contract job, I'd have said no. I took the county supervisor's job, which pleased everybody and gave me some influence for the 1952 campaign.

Immediately, I started building myself an organization. Elvie Curry, my closest friend, was the top man in it. His name was really Elva, but we always called him "Elvie." He was my third cousin, raised on the left fork of Cow Creek.

I had some others, too, almost all men who worked with me on the state roads. There was no civil service back then, so I could hire and fire who I wanted. But my road crews weren't just good politicians; the people on my team worked hard to get the work done—they all did their jobs well. For my part, I worked hard for Ray Watts, but I did it for a reason. I was holding onto that old dream I shared with my Uncle Harley Curry. Harley still lived on Cow Creek and we hadn't stopped talking about getting a road up Cow Creek Mountain.

"If we can get everybody out on election day and show us a strong precinct in here," I told Harley, "they'll have to recognize us."

I said "us"—just like Grandma.

Our part of the deal was to get Ray Watts as many votes as we could from the Island Creek district. In return, Ray would help us extend the Cow Creek road.

That road became a good issue for Ray because so many people wanted it. Plenty of folks lived on the Mingo County side of the mountain, but went to work in Logan County every day. Miners living at Monaville had to go thirty miles out of their way—through Holden, down Pidgeon Creek, and back up Rockhouse—just to get to the new mines on Island Creek. A road up Cow Creek would have shortened the trip by more than half. Ray Watts knew how much he needed me, so he agreed to get us that road once he was elected.

My lord, how we all went to work! Every Browning, Chafin, and Curry in Logan County worked politics that year. All my uncles and aunts up and down this creek—and all their families and friends—came out for Ray Watts. The ticket included him for sheriff, Chauncey Browning, Sr., for state attorney general, and, for governor, William C. Marland.

I was pretty well acquainted with Bill Marland, who was state attorney general at the time. He was a tall, handsome fellow, and a confident campaigner. It didn't matter whether Bill Marland knew you or not, he was always ready to shake your hand. He never let a minute go by without introducing himself to someone. There was no doubt in Bill Marland's mind that he was going to be this state's next governor.

Bill and Chauncey Browning were good friends, and they made appearances all up and down Island Creek. Chauncey was the best man in the world to take on a campaign around here, because Chauncey's people were all from Cow Creek. His mother, Mary, was a Curry—my mother's first cousin—so Chauncey was popular in a lot of places.

Bill Marland wasn't as well known, though, and that's where I came in. I took him and Chauncey around on our "Pony Express" route and introduced them both at all the meetings. I drove them around in McDowell County, too, which got us all known a little bit better over there.

Chauncey and Bill Marland loved campaigning. At the meetings, I gave them one hell of a good build-up—"Bill Marland: What a good man! What a good governor!"—and he liked that. He knew he had a solid team working for him in Logan County, and the same held true for Chauncey and for Ray Watts.

As primary day drew closer, it seemed like the Democrats were depending on me and my team for everything. Eventually, I felt like I was running Ray Watts's whole campaign, which wasn't easy by any means. As a candidate, Ray turned out to be missing something—a lot of people really didn't trust him. Frankly, he turned out to be almost as unpopular in the coalfields as Everett Workman had been.

Then there was the fact that Floyd Murphy, Ray's opponent, would be a tough man to beat. Floyd was fairly popular in the Logan district, which was bad enough, but he'd also been born and raised in Chapmanville. The Chapmanville district was important, and we knew that Floyd would have no trouble winning there at all. We also knew that we might be able to scare up a few votes for Ray in Chapmanville, but we had to come up with a plan to bring them out. As I've said, the best way of getting people's attention back then was to hold a political meeting. We decided to have one right in the middle of Floyd Murphy territory.

We'd been getting some road construction done around Chapmanville, and I knew a few people there. With their help, I was able to schedule a meeting at the grade school in Henlawson. Now, there was no way the people in Henlawson were going to come and listen to Ray Watts talk about Floyd Murphy, so I kept Ray's name off the agenda and played up all the other names on our ticket. I waited until about a week before the meeting before letting it out that Ray was going to be at the Henlawson meeting. I guess I should have kept it quiet a little longer. Once the word got around, it was almost like announcing that Adolf Hitler was coming in to speak. Ray must have caught wind of some trouble because he called me the night before the meeting.

"Raymond," he said, "I'm sick. I just can't go to Henlawson tomorrow. You're gonna have to speak for me."

I was disappointed, but there was nothing I could do about it. I just said, "It's OK, Ray, we'll do fine," and planned to hold the meeting without him. I didn't think there'd be any real problems.

Unfortunately, once Ray had backed down, all our other candidates decided they didn't want to go to Henlawson either. Unlike Ray, though, none of them bothered to call me up and tell me about it. This ended up putting me in something of a tight situation.

Now, Big John Chafin was my friend in those days and everybody knew he'd been one of Sheriff Don Chafin's toughest deputies in the twenties. John was getting up there in years, but he was still a big fellow—and a *mean* one. John knew the people in Henlawson, and he convinced me that I should take him along with me for protection.

"And you put you a gun in each pocket," he said. "Be damned sure you take *two;* and I'll take two myself."

"John, I don't want to kill nobody!" I told him. "That sure wouldn't do our candidates no good. . . ." But John wasn't joking.

We came to the Henlawson school that evening and there were about seventy-five people milling around outside. Right there in front, whittling on a piece of wood, was Dennis "Boss" Martin—one big, tough fellow and a strong Floyd Murphy man. Boss Martin surely was one of the meanest damned fellows in Logan County at the time, and he still is today! I looked at Boss and knew right off why he'd decided to be working away with that knife of his just then.

"Stay close to me," Big John whispered. "Boss knows what I can do."

We walked past there and went into that schoolhouse, and a good-sized crowd followed us in. (I'm pretty sure that those people counted on seeing some good fighting there that night.) John and I sat down in the front row and waited for our candidates. We waited a pretty long time but, of course, none of them was showing. There *were* no candidates; it was just me and John. Finally, I got up.

"Well, I figure it's time to start this meeting," I announced, trying to keep control of my voice. "Anybody want to open it?"

No one said a damned word.

"Well . . . I figure it's up to me, then."

I went up there and stood before all those people.

"Ladies, gentlemen," I began. "I came over here to talk to you about politics. Now, I know there's a lot of you here who ain't gonna like what I have to say. I know I'm in strong Floyd Murphy country and you might not like the people I'm for. But

I'm telling you this: You folks have drug your mufflers and tailpipes over these roads for too long a time! I know for a fact that there've been times when you couldn't even get in and out of this place, as out-of-shape as your roads are! Your schoolteacher is still afraid to drive across that old bridge outside! You didn't get a new school last year because nobody could get the materials over that bridge to build it for you! . . . I'm here to tell you that if Ray Watts is elected sheriff, we'll get you a new bridge, and we'll get your damned roads fixed too! That's the way I see it."

Of that whole damned bunch, only about twenty of them applauded. But that was enough to warm me up a little bit. I looked over at John and winked, and then I got real sweet to them.

"Now you folks can set here and do whatever you want to do. You can vote any way you like; I don't give a damn. But I'll tell you one thing. With me as chairman and Ray Watts as sheriff, there'll never be another truck coming across that rickety old bridge. . . . You be for my outfit, and I'll see that you get a new bridge, a new road, *and* a new school in the bargain!"

I said some more—I don't remember what all. But after that meeting, a lot of those people came up, wanting to shake my hand. I'd done a pretty good job at winning them over.

Suddenly John was at my side, whispering in my ear.

"Here comes Boss!" he warned. "Watch Boss! Watch him! He's a mean one!"

Dennis Martin was walking up to us. I kept looking right at him as I spoke to him.

"Boss, I know I can't change your mind," I said. "But goddamn . . . I like you anyway! Be for Floyd Murphy! Hell, I don't care! I'll still come over and fix your damned house, if you want me to!"

"Hush, goddammit," Boss Martin said, looking around. "I don't want ye convincin' *me!*"

Ray Watts didn't carry that precinct, but he came close. He won the election, and we got a new bridge for Henlawson. Afterward, we rebuilt the school and everyone was happy about that. What's more, Boss Martin and I started getting along pretty well. He and his whole family are some of the best friends I have in Logan County today.

Of course, not all election deals end up just like they're laid out. Henlawson got its roads and the bridge, but my deal for a new Cow Creek road almost ended badly for me. There's nothing like experience for teaching you, and in that election I really got crossed up. In the end, though, the cross-up turned out a good deal better for me than it did for Ray Watts.

I'd stayed with Ray, Chauncey Browning, and Bill Marland all the way through the campaign, and they all won their races. The trouble was this: Ray didn't stick with the winner. At the last minute, he ended up dropping his support for Bill Marland. Dr. H. H. Hedrick, a West Virginia congressman, had been running for governor in that primary, and he'd been supported by the United Mine Workers union. Ray Watts knew he needed the local UMW behind him for sheriff or he'd have gotten beat. So Ray *had* to go for Hedrick, although he waited until the night before the primary to announce it. Bill Marland carried every precinct that I'd set up and worked myself. But a whole lot of others in Logan County—the ones Ray had worked—went for Dr. Hedrick.

I'm telling you, it was awful. The whole state Democratic organization had been for Bill Marland—the party leaders, all the state employees on state roads, the liquor stores, and so on. Everybody had gone with Marland. But Ray Watts, the man I helped elect as sheriff, had gone over to the losing side. Chauncey Browning saw the returns and called me over to his place in Charleston.

"What in the hell happened over there, Raymond?" he asked.

"Ray Watts double-crossed me."

"You don't know Bill Marland the way I do," Chauncey said. "He'll never do a damned thing for Logan County as long as Ray's your chairman. What are you going to do?"

"Hell, I don't know."

It was true. After the election, Marland had nothing to say for Ray Watts. My problem was this: the Cow Creek road I'd promised had to be approved at the state level, and it sure didn't figure that Governor Marland was about to lay any new pavement after Ray had double-crossed him like he had.

It was the winter of 1953, and Marland had been in office for about a month. I was having lunch in Charleston with Chauncey's mother, Mary Browning, probably one of the smartest political women in the state of West Virginia. Everybody on Cow Creek knew Mary Browning as "Aunt Mary," although Chauncey called her "Gaw-gaw." She had a nice apartment on Washington Street, right across from the capitol—just about where the Department of Motor Vehicles is now.

Aunt Mary was cooking hamburgers for lunch, and I was sitting at the table with my right-hand man, Elvie Curry (her nephew), when Chauncey walked in.

"Hi, Raymond!" he said. "How you gettin' along?"

"Well, pretty good," I said. "But you know I got me a damned screwin' over there in Logan County."

Aunt Mary didn't like that kind of talk at all, and you can bet she made me apologize before going on.

"I promised them a new road up Cow Creek," I told Chauncey. "But it won't do for me to take Ray in to see the governor now! I'm almost afraid to go over there myself!"

"Wait a minute," Chauncey said. "Let me use your phone, Gaw-gaw."

He picked up the receiver and called straight over to Bill Marland's office.

"Bill?" he said. "Are you gonna to be around this afternoon? . . . What? . . . Yeah, I'm at Gaw-gaw's; she's cooking up some hamburgers. . . . Well, sure she's got extra!. . ."

Bill Marland loved Aunt Mary's cooking as much as any of us. He told Chauncey he'd be over in five minutes—and he was.

"Hi, Raymond!" he said, coming in there. "How's it goin'? You still working the state road?"

"Yes, sir."

"By God, you've got a job as long as I'm governor!"

Then Chauncey told him about my situation.

"Raymond made some political promises over there in Logan County, and you know what Ray Watts has done to us. . . ."

"To hell with Ray Watts!" Marland said. "What do you want, Raymond? Anything you say, we'll do!"

"I'd like a road up Cow Creek," I told him.

"How far is it?"

"About three miles. There's a road almost to the top of the hill, but it isn't too good."

"Well, we might be able to do that!" said Marland.

Just then, Aunt Mary came to the kitchen door with her big apron on.

"Governor," she said, "if you build that road, I'll get a big fat hen and we'll fix you some dumplings!"

Bill Marland had to smile at that.

"Then we'll just see about it, Gaw-gaw!" he winked.

After lunch, we crossed the street to the capitol and sat down in the governor's office. Bill Marland called in Burl Sawyers, the state roads commissioner. Of course, I knew Burl; I'd been working for him for some time, and he knew how badly I wanted that road. No doubt he realized what was going on just as soon as he'd walked into Marland's office and seen me there.

"Burl," said the governor, "did you ever hear of Cow Creek?"

"Hell, yes, I've heard of Cow Creek!" Burl thundered. "Raymond Chafin, I told you I'd fire you if you came around here talking up that road again!"

Everybody sitting around that room knew that Burl was kidding me. He was a good boss, and he was my friend.

"Well," said the governor, "I want a road up there and I want it started by April. Don't put it off for six months."

Not too long after that, a state survey crew came into Cow Creek. Those engineers brought in a couple of big books of blueprints and they staked out a road, complete with three or four little bridges running back and forth across the creek. They had the whole thing mapped out in two weeks.

Now, you'll remember that Harley Curry and I had been planning and surveying that road for years, all on our own. Harley and I both knew construction, and we could see how the engineers had laid out that new road. They had it going way up past a fish pond, up a whole different hollow than we wanted, and around another hill. It didn't run over Cow Creek Mountain at all—it wasn't nearly the way we'd planned it—so Harley suggested we get out there and fix it.

"Let's you and me get up there tomorrow, early in the morning," he said. "We'll stake that road out and we'll build it just the way we want it, the way it ought to be!"

Hell, that was no problem. After all, I was the county road supervisor. So Harley and I went out there and changed just about every bit of work the surveyors had done. I got me a gallon of yellow paint and every stake I could find. I took a man named Web Adams who still lives on this creek—a laborer, but a smart fellow.

"Web," I told him, "I want you to learn how to work a lock-level, and I want you to help me run a grade."

Web and I set the center stakes for that road all the way down the hill. I took the transom myself and ran the grade where Harley and I had thrashed it out.

When hiring time came around, there was no trouble finding good people to work on that road. West Virginia Coal and Coke had been hit by a market slump and was shutting down mines. Plenty of fellows had run out of unemployment and didn't have anything coming in, so I hired about thirty of them. They took crosscut saws to cut the right-of-way, and they laid the drain pipe. A couple of months later, our road was finished.

Buddy, I was really flying high with everybody around here then. Think of it: People who lived in Monaville had been going clear up to Holden, thirty-some miles to get around Logan to Mingo County. Once the new road was built, they were driving twelve. All my people—all the Currys and Brownings and Chafins along Cow Creek—prospered after that deal. They remembered what we'd done. They knew what was possible.

Robert Spence Collection, West Virginia State Archives

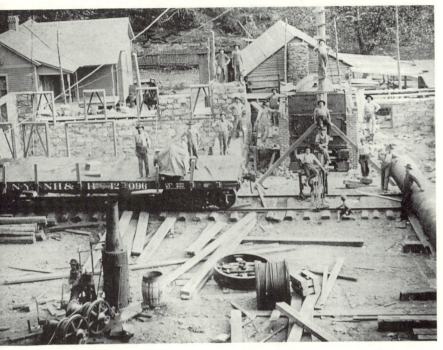

Logan County construction site around 1918.
"My daddy got back into the timber business....
He was hauling sawed lumber ... for the
railroad construction."

Omar around 1920. "There were at least ten [Junior Mercantile] stores, all in places where West Virginia Coal and Coke had mines, and they all fed out of a warehouse in Barnabus near our store at Omar."

Logan in the 1940s. "I took charge of what was left of George Steele's faction.... When the dust cleared from that election, most folks who were watching politics knew that Raymond Chafin of Logan County was someone to reckon with."

Sheriff Ray Watts (in suit) with deputies, around 1955. Okey Justice stands to the right of Watts; Blutcher Sias stands to the right of Justice. "If Ray Watts's man had been sheriff, [his deputies] would have been all over me, trying to get something on me—and on all my people, too. . . . That's the way they played it in those days."

U.S. Senator Robert C. Byrd, Raymond Chafin, and Okey Justice in 1960. "[Bob Byrd] was never a man to be pressured. Even today you can't march twenty-five or thirty people into his office and force him into doing something. He just doesn't work that way."

Left to right: Claude Ellis, Franklin Roosevelt, Jr., and Raymond Chafin. Roosevelt was campaigning for JFK in Logan, 1960. "Ray Watts's right-hand man, Claude Ellis, . . . ended up leading the local Kennedy campaign with another man, Alex DeFobio."

John F. Kennedy with reporters in the Smoke House restaurant, Logan, West Virginia. Al Otten of the *Wall Street Journal* is on the far left; Rowland Evans of the *New York Herald-Tribune* is on the far right; next to him is John Kady, United Press International. Herb Little, of the Associated Press, stands to the right and behind Kennedy. "Kennedy told the newsmen [at the Aracoma Hotel] that he was going up to get some dinner in his room and a shower before the interview [at the Smoke House]. Nobody knew it—and I was damned glad of it—but I was already up there."

Humphrey and Chafin at the Smoke House restaurant. The waitresses are Marie Mayhorn (left) and Kathy Ferrell (right). "Hubert Humphrey came to Logan and there was a dinner for him at the Smoke House. . . . Afterward I gave him the news that I'd sent his money back—all of it. 'You're not going to be against me are you?' Humphrey asked."

Ted Kennedy (holding microphone) campaigning in West Virginia with his brother John. "By the end of the campaign, the whole Kennedy family had gotten involved in West Virginia. . . . JFK's sister, . . . both his brothers, and even his mother stayed a night or two at the Aracoma."

JFK in Hinton, West Virginia. "Kennedy came to use religion to his advantage, suggesting that West Virginians might show their open-mindedness by choosing him. Once he started making those speeches, he really fired up the race—more than anybody expected."

A post-election dinner in 1960. From left: Raymond Chafin, out-going Sheriff Ed McDonald, Bus Perry, Mrs. C. C. Chambers, C. C. Chambers, and faction secretary Sylvia Vance. "[The judge] chewed us out, telling us it was all just a bunch of politics. He told us that one side was just as guilty as the other, and he threw the whole thing out of court. We left that judge's office . . . and we all had breakfast together."

8 Ray Watts and Fiddlin' Bob Byrd

SOMETIME DURING THAT SAME 1952 ELECtion campaign, I was driving along a beat-up road—a state roads project near Harts Creek—when I found a strange fellow pulled over in his old Chevrolet. He looked kind of familiar to me as he stood next to that old car with a big bass fiddle tied to the top. A glance inside told me that he had a smaller fiddle in there, too, and I kind of laughed to myself, thinking, "Now, what the hell have we got here?. . ."

But I stopped anyway; I thought he might be broken down, and I was curious.

"Hey there, buddy!" I said. "What are you doing here?"

The man smiled, reached out his hand to me, and introduced himself. "I'm Bob Byrd," he said, "and I'm running for Congress."

Then I remembered where I'd seen him before. I knew him from the state senate, where I'd been doing some lobbying. He was a senator from Raleigh County.

But meeting young Robert Byrd face-to-face on Harts Creek was another thing altogether. I looked at him and his old car with those fiddles, and I figured I'd run into a real crackpot for sure. Still, he was friendly enough—as polite a man as you could ever hope to meet.

"And what do you do for a living, sir?" he was asking me.

"I'm a state roads superintendent."

"Hey!" he said, shaking my hand again. "I'm glad to know you! A man of your caliber must have a lot of influence!"

"Now here is a fellow," I thought to myself, "who knows how to dance—and knows how to dip." I could see this right away, because I'd been dipped before!

"Yeah, well," I said cautiously, "Some of it's good and some of it's bad!"

Then I said something about wishing my influence could fix that Harts Creek road. You could hardly get a billy goat through there in those days, and there wasn't a damned thing I could do about it without some money and equipment.

But Bob Byrd was there for a different reason. He was on the campaign trail. It wasn't too long before he was asking me whether he could come by our road office to meet my workers.

"I won't campaign 'em," he assured me. "I'll just play 'em a little tune on my fiddle."

"Sure," I said. "Come over anytime you want to."

I told him the men would be at the garage the next day, if he wanted to come then. Mornings were best. There was no use to having him campaign in the evening; those fellows would have run right over top of him and his fiddles to get home.

As I drove into work, a little after six the next morning, I saw that old Chevrolet with the big bass fiddle on top. Bob Byrd was standing there waiting for me. In a few minutes, some of my men had started to drift in, and he was playing "Boil That Cabbage Down" for the early birds.

They listened to him play and a few of the old-timers even danced a step or two. He kept it up while the rest of the crew rolled in, about fifty people working there all together. Then we had to get off to work.

"Let's line 'em up now, boys," I said, and the senator thanked me before taking off down the road.

About two o'clock that afternoon, Ray Watts called me up. Aside from me working on his campaign for sheriff, Ray was the Logan County Democratic chairman.

"Hey Chafe!" he said. "Did you have a feller name of Byrd up there playin' his fiddle this morning?"

"Yeah!"

"Damn, buddy!" he said. "That S.O.B. don't have no money! He can't help us!"

"Well, I don't know, Ray," I said. "He plays that fiddle pretty good. You ought to come up there and listen to him."

I said that because I liked Bob Byrd. I liked his politicking. Besides—and I didn't tell Ray this—I'd already started helping him out. I had told him he could come and play that fiddle for my men "anytime."

Ray came up, and we had a big discussion about the musical senator from Raleigh County.

"That man could help you," I told him. "He has a fiddle and he knows how to use it. He can get out on that street and gather up a whole mess of people in about ten minutes. If you're smart, you'll step out there and introduce him! I'm telling you, Ray, if you don't get him, Floyd Murphy will."

"Can he really play it?"

"He sure as hell can," I said. "I'd introduce him myself, but I'd get in trouble with my job. Don't let Floyd get him, Ray."

The next time Bob Byrd came around, Ray and I caught up with him at Barnabus where he was playing in Parlee Chambers's store. Her old man, Bill Chambers, was a fiddler too, and they had all kinds of people in there listening to Bob Byrd play. He could play just about anything they asked, and pretty soon there were more people in that store than there was room to hold.

When he was done, Ray and I walked up to him. "Senator," I said, "I'd like you to meet Ray Watts, our candidate for sheriff."

Byrd was too smart to get mixed up in any factional fights, and he kind of backed away from me then. When I explained that Ray was also the Democratic chairman in Logan County, the senator relaxed a little.

"If you take that fiddle and meet Ray on the steps of the county courthouse this evening," I said, "you might draw yourself a pretty good crowd."

"Sure," said Ray. "I'll introduce you. Come on down there later!"

That afternoon, I mustered a bunch of people myself at that courthouse, bringing my road crew and some others to help get things started. Bob Byrd showed up, Ray introduced him, and before it was all over, the crowd had grown to over a hundred people.

"I'm not going to make a campaign speech," Byrd told them. "I just want you all to remember one thing. I'm Bob Byrd, and I'm running for Congress. My name will be on the ballot 'Robert Byrd' B-*Y*-R-D!"

They gave him a big hand when he said that, and then Ray got up there to talk.

"Boy, he looks like he'd make a real good congressman, don't he?"

As the campaign went on, I helped Bob Byrd by telling him where he could find more people to play for. I sent him around to the different post offices on Island Creek, and sometimes I even went ahead of him to tell folks that he was coming. He campaigned all over Logan County, playing that fiddle everywhere he went. Of course, he won the election here; he just swamped this county. In my precinct at Barnabus, I believe he got 98 percent of the vote.

I always liked Bob because he talked to you. He was never a man to be pressured. Even today, you can't march twenty-five or thirty people into his office and force him into doing something. He just doesn't work that way. He talks to people individually. He's a straight-shooter. I've always found him to be like that.

I've got one more "little one" to tell on Bob Byrd. For some time, we'd been trying to get a new courthouse in Logan County. In 1960, it came to a question of getting the right federal funds, and I called him about it.

"Raymond," he told me. "You go see the president. You tell him *I'll* support him if he helps get you that courthouse—and he's going to need me."

A few days later, someone from John Kennedy's office called me with a message. "The senator and the president have talked," they said. "And you're going to get your courthouse."

I was always one for a little fun, so I asked, "Which senator would that be?" Of course I knew before they told me.

But this is getting ahead of things.

After that 1952 campaign, I became more active in Logan County politics. In 1956, I was elected to the county Democratic Executive Committee and we voted Ray Watts out as chairman. We put a couple of other people in the leadership, but none of them worked out, so I took the chairmanship over sometime in '56 or '57.

By 1958, I really was working hard at it. We decided we wanted a man named Okey Hager on the County Commission,[1] and Ray Watts, who was still on the commission himself, told us he would stand behind Okey. Then he turned around and

1. Chafin actually calls the three-member County Commission the "County Court," a term handed down from the British colony of Virginia. We're calling it the "County Commission" throughout the book for the sake of consistency.—T. S.

double-crossed us again; Ray went for Okey Justice and, together, they beat Okey Hager.

Goddamn, but that irritated me! Ray had left me hanging out to dry in the very same way he'd done during Bill Marland's race in '52!

"Well, well, well," I thought. "I'll just wait for you, young man!"

I began to see that Ray Watts was trying to keep everything just the way he wanted it—holding his controlling influence on the County Commission and his power to name election officers. The election officers were still vital to any election. You really needed them to win. Ray had all the marbles.

As good a politician as he was, though, Ray didn't know how powerful we were. He didn't go back to the precincts and see the organization we had out there. He wanted to hold onto things, but he couldn't go on saying one thing, doing another, and still expect to succeed. He'd won Okey Justice for that commission seat—but only by a few votes. I told my people to wait it out. "Okey Justice is good enough," I said. "Let's support him and bide our time."

In 1959, Ray was still sitting pretty. He had a good hold on the County Commission, the sheriff's office, and substantial influence over the Democratic Executive Committee. Then some cracks started appearing in his organization.

Ray's brother-in-law, R. J. Cook, was on the commission, but R. J. wanted to be sheriff. Ray promised to help him win that office. Then, Ray turned around and told R. J. to stay on the commission. Instead, Ray decided to run for sheriff himself—having sat out for four years.

All this didn't go too well with me and my group because we liked R. J. Cook. We saw it as another way that Ray Watts had double-crossed someone.

I sat in my office thinking about all this one day when I

thought I might have a way to get even with Mr. Watts. "By God," I thought. "I've got to figure this out." I went to my good friend and right-hand man, Elvie Curry.

"Elvie," I said, "Let's take a drive up Cow Creek where we can think."

They tell me that Elvie was the only member of my bunch who could really talk to me. I took him everywhere, although I almost had to tie him up to get him on an airplane once.

He had made straight A's in school, but Elvie never could get a job from anyone. He was a good worker; he just could never walk up to someone and ask them for a job. I got him the first job he ever had in his life—as a clerk at the Junior Mercantile store—and practically every one after that.

But what Elvie had was an amazing political sense. He always liked soft-soled shoes, and it was just like he could slip through a crowd without anyone knowing he was there. He could work his way around that room and never say a word, his mind clicking all the time. When he came out of there, Elvie Curry could give me a perfect picture of what was going on.

So Elvie and I went up to Cow Creek that day and we talked about Ray Watts and his dealings with Okey Justice and the Hagers, the main political rivals in Chapmanville.

Red Hager was one of the best politicians in Chapmanville. His people had held just about every major political office down there. Red and his father, Okey Hager, hated Okey Justice with a passion. The Hagers and Justices would have liked to cut one another's head off. But they all had something against Ray Watts. The Hagers were still mad at Ray for double-crossing them and going with Okey Justice as county commissioner.

For his part, Okey J. had done well by Ray, because Ray had helped him win a seat on the County Commission. But I knew that Okey really wanted to be sheriff. Ray had promised to help him win the sheriff's office—in four years, after he himself was done with it. This is what Elvie and I were talking about on Cow Creek.

"Elvie," I said, "Do you think we might get Okey Justice to work with the Hagers against Ray?"

Elvie thought about it a minute.

"You know," he said at last, "They say you can do just about anything if you set your mind to it—and if you work hard enough."

"I can't do it by myself," I said. "I need you and the others helping me."

"Damn, Raymond," he said, "I wouldn't know where to start!"

We started by going to Red Hager, who was my friend and a member of my group. Red's wife, Elizabeth, was also on the Democratic Executive Committee.

"Red," I asked, "How would you like to get even with Ray Watts?"

"You bet I would!"

"Do you think you could ever get together with Okey Justice?"

"Hell, no! That son-of-a-bitch beat my daddy!"

"Hold on, there!" I said, and I called Elvie in to back me up. We both told Red how much political "clout" we'd have if everybody pulled together.

"If we can bring on Okey Justice, we'd beat the hell out of Ray Watts," we told Red. "We could take the commission! We already have Red Bivens for us as it is! If we had Okey, we'd have the whole thing!"

"Well, you go find out what Okey Justice has to say about it," said Red. "And we'll see. . ."

Elvie Curry and I went to see Okey Justice that very night. We waited until two o'clock in the morning, when no one would know what we were doing. Elvie drove me over to Okey's and waited in the car down the road. I went up to the Justice place and knocked on that door. I heard Okey's voice from somewhere inside.

"Who is it?" he called.
"It's Raymond Chafin!"
"What the hell do *you* want?"
"I want to talk to you!"

Then I heard Nola, Okey's wife, ordering him to let me in.

"We don't run nobody from *our* front door!" she said. "You let him in, and you talk to him!"

Okey opened the door. He practically filled the doorway—a big, tall country fellow, he was. He stood there in his long nightshirt, which made him look for all the world like an old country sheriff. His wife got up and fixed us each a sandwich.

"I'm here to make a deal," I said. "You know, you folks were wading across this creek until I came in here and built that road behind your house. I built those two bridges out there too. . . ."

I had his attention.

"You know that Raymond Chafin gets things done for you, and you know I've always done what I promised! Right now, Okey, I want to make you sheriff!"

On hearing that, Okey Justice got out of his chair, tugging at that gown of his a time or two. He was thinking hard about what I'd said. Eventually, he mentioned that Ray Watts had promised to help him become sheriff the next time around.

"But that's four years away, Okey! I'm willing to make you sheriff now!"

We talked more as we ate our sandwiches. Eventually, I went out and called Elvie in. (Elvie had married a Justice, so Okey and his wife knew him well.) We laid out the plan for them: Okey would run against Ray and cooperate with the Hagers, his political rivals in Chapmanville.

"Do you think you can get along with them?" I asked.

Okey wanted to know whether I'd talked to them yet.

"Now, Okey," I said. "If you don't ask me any questions, I won't have to lie to you!"

He thought some more.

"Well, I figure I might get along with them all right!" he said. "What would we have to do?"

"By God, you've got to be with Raymond Chafin!" I told him. "And I've got to be the one running the show! If you go to fooling around with it and making deals on your own, the whole thing goes down the drainpipe...."

In the end, Okey Justice got with us. Then we went to Okey Hager, Red's daddy, and told him we could put him on the County Commission if *he* could get with us. A commission spot would be open—just as soon as our new candidate, Okey Justice, left it to become sheriff.

What a job of selling that was! But when we got through, the Hagers, Okey Justice, and everybody agreed to cooperate—just because Ray Watts had double-crossed so many of them.

In the meantime, I'd been working in Sharples for the Boone County Coal Company. Another outfit, Omar Mining, had been asking me to come back and work on a project of theirs near Barnabus. I welcomed the chance to move back because Louise and I didn't like it where we were. Also, the move would have allowed me to be closer to the next election—the election of 1960.

By January of that year, I thought I had everything set. About that same time, a certain U.S. senator from Massachusetts was on the campaign trail. He thought he had everything "set" in West Virginia, too. We were both wrong on that point. Jack Kennedy and I were in for a much bigger political fight in West Virginia than either of us had ever figured on.

9 Kennedy

HUBERT HUMPHREY MOVED INTO SOUTHERN West Virginia faster than Kennedy's people did. Early on, some powerful Democrats in Charleston were looking at Humphrey and liking what they saw. Before the last snow had fallen in Logan, one of his men had contacted my faction and donated two thousand dollars to our campaigns.

On April 11, 1960, about a month before the state primary, we set up Humphrey with a big breakfast in downtown Logan. We filled the big hall over the radio station and served bacon and eggs to three hundred people, a breakfast that cost us around four hundred dollars all together.

I was the county Democratic chairman, but I didn't introduce any of the speakers at the breakfast that morning, not even Humphrey. That would have implied my support, and it was still too early for that. For me, the best thing at that point was to sit back and watch the crowds—to see how they listened to this fellow or that one.

Humphrey and his wife, Muriel, spoke—along with some of our local candidates. He talked about unemployment and said a lot of good things that our people wanted to hear. There were certainly plenty of folks behind him that day, and I felt good about supporting him.

I still felt that way by the time the Kennedys came in here and started spending a little money. Their people came to me, but I'd already accepted Humphrey's two thousand, and nobody thought John F. Kennedy could win anyway. They couldn't get me to be with them, so they went to Ray Watts, who still controlled several votes on the executive committee.

Ray said "no" to them too. I think he was afraid to be for JFK at that time because, as I said, nobody thought he could win. The next one they went to was Ray's right-hand man, Claude Ellis, and Claude said he'd help Kennedy in Logan County. Claude ended up leading the local Kennedy campaign with another man, Alex DeFobio.

I didn't pay too much attention to them, though. I was busy putting my own organization together. One fellow I worked real hard to get with me was county judge C. C. "Cush" Chambers, who I wanted to run for reelection. Judge Chambers was a grouchy old fellow with a long history in Logan County. He was an old friend of George Steele's, and I'd worked on his campaigns in the past, so the judge agreed to get with my ticket. Judge Chambers was the anchor of my slate—him and Glenn Jackson, who was running for reelection as state senator. I also had Oval Damron running for county prosecutor. Without these men, I wouldn't have had any faction at all.

Still, I don't mind saying that keeping this bunch together was the biggest challenge of my political career. Some of my people (like the Hagers) didn't trust Okey Justice; Okey didn't especially like some of them either, and Judge Chambers was a man who was just plain hard to like—although I did. I had to keep on top of all these men and make them quit fighting each other. I needed them to help each other politically, and "talk nice" about one another before crowds and out on the street.

"The first time I hear of any trouble," I told them, "Off comes somebody's head!"

But, for all their differences, all my main candidates did have one thing in common. None of them liked U.S. Senator John F. Kennedy. None of them thought a Catholic could win the presidency; and none of them thought he had any business in the White House. They were real strong on Hubert Humphrey, and this was something that pulled them all together.

Almost a week after the breakfast for Humphrey, John Kennedy started campaigning in West Virginia. His people invited party leaders from all over the state to come in and meet with him in Charleston. As Democratic chairman in Logan, I was invited to the Daniel Boone Hotel, where Kennedy and his people were staying. I knew I couldn't support him, but I was curious to see what the man was like, so I drove up there with Glenn Jackson, our candidate for reelection to the state senate. Glenn had been the previous chairman of the County Executive Committee, and he was a powerful senator, so Kennedy's people thought he'd be a good one to bring in that day.

They were wrong on that score. Glenn was a good politician, but he was a bad choice for Kennedy because—like Judge Chambers and some of my other candidates—Glenn was a Mason. In my part of the country at that time, the Masons wanted absolutely nothing to do with Catholics—and surely not one as president.

Glenn and I stepped onto the mezzanine just above the lobby, and we looked around. Kennedy's campaign had pretty much taken the place over. The mezzanine was filled with people talking about this and that. Many of them were state politicians who'd already committed themselves to Kennedy and just wanted the chance to shake his hand. The senator's aides were all over the place, directing people this way and that.

For his part, Kennedy never seemed to be by himself. He had at least two or three aides in the room with him all the time, plus some others outside. I counted some fifteen or twenty people with him that day, and he hadn't even won the primary yet!

Glenn and I were brought in there and, because I'd never been to a meeting quite like this, I pretty much just wanted to sit back and let him talk. Glenn started in and, almost immediately, hung himself.

"Do you think you can win this election," he asked, "being a Catholic?"

Well, I could see that nobody there cared to hear that kind of talk. It didn't sound just right to them, or maybe they'd noticed Glenn's Mason ring. But it seemed like Glenn had turned the light right off himself with that question. One or two of Kennedy's aides stepped up beside him and very politely asked, "Senator, do you mind if we discuss this with Mr. Jackson a minute?" Kennedy nodded, and they worked Glenn right on out of there.[1]

I was impressed at how smart that was, taking a person out of the way like that without making him mad or anything. They really had some organization, and that's just what beat Hubert Humphrey in the end. The Kennedys were so powerful and so smart, politically.

So, after Glenn was hustled out of there, I was left with Kennedy, and he asked for my support. I had to be honest with him.

"I'm already obligated," I told him. "But whoever wins the primary, I'll be for them in the general."

"Well, do you have any feelings against me personally?" he asked.

---

1. Glenn was on my slate, but he wasn't really a team player. He'd been in the state senate for years and he thought he knew everything about politics, but he had another think coming. Glenn stayed on with Hubert Humphrey. He campaigned on his own, linking his opponent to Kennedy—and that boomeranged on him. It got him beat.

"No," I said. "As far as I know, you're all right."

He smiled at that, and he was as nice as he could be about it—not angry at all. Actually, he reminded me of myself when someone had to tell me "no" sometimes.

We stood up and shook hands, and I'll never forget that handshake. Later I mentioned it to my friends, wishing I had a handshake as warm as that.

"There are so many things I could do for West Virginia," Kennedy said as I was leaving. "I really hope you can support me in the future—and that I can be your president."

"Well, I'm sorry," I said. "I just can't do it now."

I wished him well and left. We hadn't talked for very long, but, in those few minutes with him, John Kennedy had really gone a long way to selling me on himself. Then I met his wife, and she did at least as much, if not more.

Jackie Kennedy was sitting alone at a desk outside. It seemed like nobody else was paying much attention to her, so I sat with her and we ended up talking for some time.

She was very much down-to-earth—maybe a little bit more so than her husband. He had talked about politics, about government, poverty, unemployment, and so on. But Mrs. Kennedy, who was just thirty years old at the time, talked more about things that a parent would be interested in. She spoke about her children, schools, and other things that we needed in West Virginia, and I could see that she was very interested in our state. It was my impression that she really cared about things that were happening here.

Don't get me wrong; Jackie Kennedy could talk politics just like her husband. She knew a great deal about politics. She said she wanted to be a "working first lady," and I suggested she might become another Eleanor Roosevelt.

"Oh, don't expect that," she said. "No one could ever replace her!"

I came away from that meeting extremely impressed with the Kennedys as people and as politicians—and I mean *both* of them.

In those days, my organization consisted of two groups. First, there were the people out in the various neighborhoods, who acted kind of like our field advisors. We listened to them and they told us what they thought we should do about this or that, and a lot of them ended up working the precincts for us on election day. Then, I had a small team, a core group of fellows who worked more closely with me. We held regular meetings, and we talked about things, arguing and fussing with each other about precinct captains and so on. Entire elections turned on what we decided in those meetings.

Elvie Curry was still with me. Good old Elvie, my best friend, who always had a smile on his face and was never without a good word to say. Steady is what Elvie was; if you met him twenty times a year, he'd be the same man every time, friendly and laid-back—but rougher than hell if you ever locked horns with him.

If Elvie was the nicest fellow in our bunch, Arnold Harkins was the toughest. A tall man with big shoulders, Arnold favored suits and a smart shine on his shoes. Arnold had been a deputy sheriff; he'd worked for the school board and the state liquor commission. Arnold was a smart cookie, and he knew a lot of folks. That knowledge made him a good one for picking election officers.

Arnold made it his job to let us know when somebody wasn't doing what they'd said they were going to do. If we thought one of our people wasn't helping us just right, Arnold went out and reminded them of what we'd done for them. He didn't mince words, either. Nine times out of ten, after a visit from Arnold, that person practically tore down my door to find out what he'd done wrong. We didn't threaten anyone physically. We didn't thump people or kill anyone, like they did in the old days. People wanted to stay on our side because of what we did *for* them—not against them.

Red Hager ran the Chapmanville district for me. Red was named for his hair, and maybe a little bit for his temper too. He was a short, stocky fellow and a smart politician—one of the best maneuverers in the world. But Red had a big heart, and he was a war hero; he'd fought in World War I and was hit by shrapnel. The scars on his chest were with him for life.

Jack Ferrell was at some of our meetings, but not all of them. He was a young man who had been trying to get his wife on the Democratic Executive Committee. Having someone on the committee was real important to us, so Jack and I agreed to team up. I helped elect his wife, and Jack became our organization's treasurer.

Finally, we started inviting a man named Lester Perry into our meetings. "Bus" Perry was a big fellow with a ready smile. He'd been friends with some of the fellows in Ray Watts's faction, but he also supported one or two of our candidates, so Bus started getting involved with us. My sense at the time, though, was that Ray had sent Bus over to keep an eye on us. I didn't invite him to all our meetings—not in the beginning at least.

That was basically my "inner team," the ones who helped me run our candidates and the ones I reported to when I got back from that April meeting with Kennedy in Charleston. Elvie Curry was especially interested in hearing about JFK, and he made no secret about how he favored him in the primary.

"You know, Raymond," he said, "You're gonna have a hell of a time getting me off him."

My first thought was to send my best friend Elvie, who liked Kennedy anyway, to help "Big Claude" Ellis with their campaign. Claude was lined up with Ray Watts, and I would have given anything to know what Claude and Ray were doing about the local races. I hinted at it to Elvie.

"Oh, no-o," he said, backing off. "I ain't doing that for you!"
We talked some more, and someone suggested trying to sour Kennedy's people on Claude Ellis. "If we talk to those Kennedys about Claude, they just might quit him."

At that point, I became a little afraid to say anything with Bus Perry around. He still favored some of Ray Watts's candidates, and I really didn't know where he stood with us.

"Boys," I said, "Let's adjourn. I've got a headache; I ought to get on home."

Later that evening, I called my closest members together (leaving Bus out), and we met at Arnold Harkins's place, under the big apple tree in his yard.

Elvie spoke up. "You know you made me madder than hell this evening, asking me to go over to the other side."

He was really angry about it—what we call "Curry mad."

"And I'm gonna tell you something," he said. "You'd better just leave Claude Ellis be. You'd best let those Kennedys have him. If they get rid of him, he'll just go to fighting us, and then we'll get our ticket beat! Leave him over there! Let him go after their money. That way he'll leave us alone!"

Elvie was right about that, and we decided to leave Claude to the Kennedys for the whole campaign. I even had people building Claude up a little bit ("Goddamn, he's tough, isn't he?"). We didn't care if he and Ray got a few thousand dollars for their races—as long as we won Judge Chambers and Okey Justice for sheriff. Hell, John F. Kennedy could take care of himself—and we still didn't think he could win.

Your candidates aren't worth a nickel if they don't win, so my group planned everything. Fifty votes could make or break a race. Even ten votes could mean a whole night's work to us sometimes. Many was the night that we stayed up, fussing over the best moves to make—even on just one question!

People voted in blocks back then. Whole families got together on who to vote for, and, naturally, they went with the candidate who could do the most for them. If you got one man with you, most times you were talking about his whole family and friends too. People were familiar with my slate—the list of candidates my faction supported. If one of our people had gotten something done for one man or one community, they all knew it. I didn't have to buy their votes. Hell, most times I didn't even have to go visit them.[2]

After the election, people knew where to go when they wanted something. I got things done for them. I helped them get jobs, or roads, or helped them get their benefits. I did things for people on the other side, too, not just my own. After all, someone who's against you today might be for you tomorrow.

Kennedy and Humphrey had just come out of the Wisconsin primary. They both wanted—and needed—a big win in West Virginia's run-off, set for May 10. Kennedy had been confident early on, but selling Appalachian mountaineers on himself turned out to be a bigger job than he'd figured. What bothered people most was the religion issue—not just here, but in other states too.

In West Virginia back then, Protestants outnumbered Catholics at least twenty to one, and the Kennedys didn't quite know how to handle that. Sometime in mid-April, they decided to tackle the issue head-on.

"Nobody asked me if I was a Catholic when I joined the United States Navy," he told one crowd. "Did forty million Americans lose their right to run for the presidency on the day

2. I'm not saying that vote-buying didn't happen in 1960—a vote could be bought for two dollars, a drink of whiskey, or a whole pint. More often than not, it was something that was controlled at the precinct level.

they were baptized as Catholics? . . . Nobody asked my brother if he was a Catholic or a Protestant before he climbed into an American bomber plane to fly his last mission."

Kennedy came to use the religion issue to his advantage, suggesting that West Virginia voters might show their open-mindedness by choosing him. Once he started making those speeches, he really fired up the race—more than anybody expected.

By this time, my group had started meeting in a couple of rooms we had in the Aracoma Hotel. On one particular day, we gathered in room 220, a big room with plenty of chairs. We sat around in there, smoking cigarettes and talking politics. Bus Perry and I talked about his son Chuck, a college boy who was home for spring vacation. Chuck had been there, in our "office," the day before. He'd been talking about Kennedy, saying how all the young people at the university were for him.

"You-all'd better get on the ball!" he told us.

This was still in my head, and I figured on using it to needle Bus a little bit. "It looks like your boy's really sold on Kennedy," I started. "Says he's gonna win. . . . How are you and Ethel takin' that?"

"Well," said Bus, "Ethel believes in him too! She thinks Kennedy just might be the one to 'straighten this country out.' "

"Sounds to me like Chuck's got more control over his mother than you do," I suggested.

Bus jumped up at that, shoved his hands into his pockets, and walked around the room a couple of times. "You think my boy's smarter than I am?" he asked.

Elvie, who was already out in the open for Kennedy, spoke up. "It might just pay for us to listen to your boy, Bus," he said.

This is how our conversations went, although we couldn't talk like that when our candidates were around. They were mostly older men, and strongly against Kennedy. No matter how wrong they might have been, I still had to listen to these fellows. I needed them. Without them—Judge Chambers, Okey Justice, Oval Damron, and Glenn Jackson—I wouldn't have had a ticket or a faction. Still, with younger folks like Bus's boy starting to speak up, I began to wonder whether I might be wrong, whether we all were wrong. My wheels started turning on that senator with the nice handshake.

One other thing happened to make me think twice about Kennedy's chances in West Virginia, this time involving the man who employed me. I had taken the local job as a superintendent for Omar Mining Company, then owned by Morgan Massey, a big coal operator around here. Morgan knew about my political activity, and he didn't discourage it. In fact, my work for him included political consulting and lobbying. For the 1960 primary, the company gave me time off to handle my campaigns, and Morgan Massey liked to keep up with what I was doing.

"Raymond," he said, "Are you still against Kennedy?"

"It looks like I'm gonna have to be," I told him, referring to my candidates.

"You know," he said, "I don't like to fool with politics. I don't care who's president myself, but I think he'd be the best man for us. He'd be good for the coal business."

From this, I realized that Morgan Massey, my employer, would have liked for me to be for Kennedy too. He knew he couldn't pressure me but here, again, was somebody for JFK—and a businessman at that!

Sometime after that, I took a little poll and contacted some of the political leaders I knew in five or six other southern West Virginia counties. I wanted to know how the presidential race looked in their territory.

"Boy, I'm kind of stumped over here!" I told them. "How's this fellow Humphrey doing with you?"

They said, generally, that Hubert Humphrey had started out all right. He'd weakened some since the beginning of the campaign.

"What about Kennedy?"

In almost every case, religion came up. The other county leaders had the same thing that we did in Logan: a lot of holiness churches—fundamentalists—and most of these people just didn't know what to make of Kennedy's Catholicism.

On April 25, John Kennedy got himself a big tour bus to carry him and his people through southern West Virginia. He came through McDowell County—through Ieager and up Island Creek—making speeches and shaking hands the whole way through. When they hit Omar, somebody had set up a place in the parking lot of Shaheen's Shopping Center for him to talk.

My wife took our daughter, Margaret, who was about eleven years old at the time, and they went down there to hear Senator Kennedy speak. They had timed the rally with a shift change at the mines, so there were scores of miners in their work clothes listening to JFK talk about West Virginia. There were some two hundred people in that crowd but, of all people, a local photographer chose to zero-in on Louise and Margaret, my wife and daughter. Snap-snap-snap.

That week, the picture ended up in a local newspaper; there they were, right in there with John F. Kennedy. It caused me no end of talk. "Raymond Chafin's family at a *Kennedy* rally." People were saying Louise and Margaret had made the headlines while I'd made the funny papers. I didn't fuss about it too much, though. That's politics, and Louise sure wasn't about to change her mind about Jack Kennedy.

"I wanted to hear him," she told me. "And I *like* him!"

By the time Kennedy came to Logan, though, I was a busy man, not getting too much sleep. All my political maneuverings had won me the power to name *all* the Democratic election officers in the county—two-hundred-some poll workers in eighty-three precincts—and that was no easy job.

Nothing was more important to a politician than the power to name the people who worked inside the "houses," and these were decisions that kept me up late that spring. I had to name election officers who I knew would be with us, people who couldn't be bought by the other candidates or factions.

I'm not going to lie to you. Things hadn't changed that much since 1936. Election officers were still glad to help voters whenever they needed it.

"Those boys in each house are known as the Lever Brothers," one local fellow told *Life* magazine that year. "And, man, on Election Day they play the levers in those voting machines like 'Auld Lang Syne!' "

It's not fair to say that all election workers were "Lever Brothers," but I can tell you that there's some truth to that story. In any case, it's fair to say that I held most of the cards for the 1960 primary in Logan County, and everybody knew it. Kennedy's people found out, and they wanted me on their side. They'd been working on me for some time before he came to Logan, and they were still at it when he got there.

He'd been touring around with his bus that day, and he stopped to spend the night in Logan. Of all places, they checked him into our own Aracoma Hotel—home to room 220, the Chafin-faction office. About two o'clock that afternoon, Kennedy's people came to me and asked whether I couldn't talk with their candidate again. I said I would, and they took me upstairs to his room.

Kennedy had been speaking at the county courthouse that day and was scheduled for a radio interview at the Smoke House restaurant that night. He told the newsmen downstairs that he was going up to get some dinner in his room and a shower before the interview. Nobody knew it—and I was damned glad of it—but I was already up there. He walked in, we shook hands, and we talked alone for about twenty minutes.

"I've heard that you have more influence here than anyone else," he said. "I'd appreciate your support in this primary."

I admitted it was true. I also told him what I'd been telling some of his aides all along. It was my feeling that the people he'd gotten with in West Virginia—the ones I knew about—cared more about feathering their own nests than about national politics.

"They don't care whether you're president or not," I told him. "They just want your money to run their campaigns. They're glad to be taking whatever you've got—and you could still end up with nothing."

He asked me why I couldn't help him in West Virginia, and I said I would have liked to have been for him, "But the people I'm with, they're for the other man."

I told him how things worked in this part of the country. I admitted not knowing whether he could win; I told him I didn't know too much about national politics.

"And, to tell you the truth," I said, "I'm not that interested in it. It don't matter to me whether you or Humphrey is president. I don't think your race is going to mean a whole lot to us either way."

Hearing this, Jack Kennedy really let go on me.

"That's where you're wrong!" he said. "I'll mean more to you in West Virginia than anyone else in this race. I'll do more here because I've been here and I've seen how much you people need."

He said he'd met coal miners who told him something about health and safety in the mines. He'd been touring all through the southern mountains, where people were hard hit by poverty and unemployment. He got me to talking, too—about the roads and the dams we needed for flood control. Finally, Senator Kennedy of Massachusetts made me a promise.

"If I become president," he said, "I'll talk with you personally in Washington. You and I will sit down, and we'll discuss getting something done about these problems in southern West Virginia."

This worked. He sold me. How could I not be sold on him? From that point on, I wanted John F. Kennedy to be president, and I told him so. I didn't know how I was going to do it, but I was going to try and help him win.

"One thing, though," I said. "We can't tell anyone we ever met here tonight."

"It'll be between you and me," John Kennedy said. "We won't discuss it."

10 The 1960 Election

BY THE END OF APRIL, THE PRESIDENTIAL race had grown from a thorn to a lance in my side. Kennedy—especially after his visit—was more popular around here than ever before. And now I was even for him! But my main candidates were stronger than ever for Hubert Humphrey.

Imagine how hard this was for me, how complicated it was! All my top candidates, who didn't really like each other very much, had one thing in common: they were all for Hubert Humphrey. And here I was, committed to helping the other fellow win!

The sheriff, the prosecutor, and the judge—I *had* to win those races. I would have been in deep trouble even if just one of them got beat. If Ray Watts's man had been sheriff, for example, they would have been all over me, trying to get something on me—and on all my people, too. Ray and his bunch would have done anything in the world to cut me out of power and keep me down. That's the way they played it in those days. I would have given up my job to win that election. Hell, I could get another job! But how could I win my reputation and my influence back?

THE 1960 ELECTION

So, with everything heating up the way it was, I decided I needed help. I needed to bring someone into the leadership right next to me, a right-hand man. I discussed it with Elvie, but he said he didn't want the job. We needed someone who would be good with people and who'd be a good speaker. Of my whole group, the most obvious choice turned out to be Bus Perry.

Now, from the start, I knew that someone had likely sent Bus over to watch us; but I'd been watching him myself since then. I'd watched him at our meetings, and I'd seen him working hard on our campaigns. Bus had openly dropped his support for a couple of Ray Watts's people, and he'd even told me he thought we were going to win Judge Chambers and Oval Damron as prosecutor. One day after discussing it with Elvie, I called Bus into room 220 at the Aracoma.

"Now, I know why you came in with us," I told him. "Don't you think for a minute that I don't have my own people out there doing the same thing for me."

I told Bus I wanted him for the second spot in our organization.

"But if you double-cross me, if you cause me to lose this thing," I said, "I'll kill you."

Bus just grinned at that. "I wouldn't blame you neither," he said. "But, buddy, you're gonna win this thing! And I'm with you all the way!"

With Bus out in front with me, we had about the best organization possible. He was well educated, and he had guts and political savvy like nobody else. You could be calling Bus a son-of-a-bitch today, and he'd be posing in the same group photo with you tomorrow. I could put him anywhere, and he'd always shine. Bus was smarter than I was, in a way, but he never wanted to take the lead. He was always the man behind the man, the assistant. He'd been the majority whip in the state house of delegates, and he could have been governor, if he'd wanted it.

A day or so after I met with John Kennedy in the Aracoma, a man walked up to me outside the Smoke House restaurant and introduced himself as Jim McCahey. Mr. McCahey was some kind of coal buyer from Chicago—one of the biggest ones around, so they told me—and a strong Kennedy man. He bought coal from Island Creek Coal Company and several others around here, so that made him someone the coal companies would listen to.[1]

Any good salesman is usually a good buyer—and a good mixer. The buyer knows what he wants and knows how to find it. He knows the quality of what he's getting. A good mixer knows how to bring people together. Jim McCahey was both buyer and mixer. He knew he wanted me on his side, and he knew how to get me together with the people I needed.

We sat down, and McCahey didn't waste any time working on me to be for Kennedy. I told him about Hubert Humphrey and the two thousand dollars he'd given us.

"I can't accept his money and not be for him," I said.

"Well, then, take two thousand from us and send it back," McCahey said. That was the first money I accepted from the Kennedy campaign. We got it from them and sent it right back to Humphrey's people.

My sense has been that McCahey liked me, not just because I was helping his candidate, but because I was honest and told him the truth. I never talked anyone down or tried to cut anyone out. In fact, I even told him that Claude Ellis was a good man for them to have on board.

"And if *we* get together for you," I said, "You've got it *all.*"

---

1. James McCahey, Jr., is identified in Dan B. Fleming, *Kennedy vs. Humphrey, West Virginia 1960*, as president of the Dunn Coal Company, working in the West Virginia campaign for Sargent Shriver. McCahey, who had also worked for Dan Daley's mayoral campaign in Chicago, later became a vice-president of the C&O Railroad.—T. S.

THE 1960 ELECTION

In return, I asked for two things. That Kennedy's people keep my support quiet and that they keep Claude Ellis real busy so he'd have less time to work on our local races. I couldn't tell anyone about my work with the Kennedy campaign, not even my closest people, not yet. If word had gotten out that I was for JFK, my own candidates would have turned against me in a minute, and that would have sunk the whole boat. We kept Humphrey's posters up, but we were with him in name only.

Later that week, Hubert Humphrey came to Logan and there was a dinner for him at the Smoke House. His speech didn't go over too well with the crowd, and afterward I gave him the news that I'd sent his money back—all of it.

"You're not going to be against me are you?" Humphrey asked.

I told him I just couldn't afford to get mixed up in the presidential race, that it was splitting my people up too much. He must have understood what I was talking about. The race had become real bitter by then—for everyone. You couldn't hardly pick up a newspaper without somebody saying how they wished all the presidential politics would just go away. Humphrey knew exactly what I was talking about.

Meanwhile, the election was less than two weeks away and Jim McCahey was moving fast. The day after we met, he set up a meeting at the offices of Island Creek Coal Company, one of the biggest operations in Logan County, if not the state. I needed Island Creek's support for my local candidates, and McCahey was helping me get it. The company had been backing Ray Watts for sheriff, and their employees counted for a lot of votes. As a major customer, McCahey's word counted among Island Creek's executives.

"We're here to talk business," he told the man sitting there with us that day. "I'm not interested in local politics, only in the presidency." He added that it was in the company's interest to be concerned about the presidential race too. He made it clear to them that I was the man whose influence he wanted. He asked whether Island Creek had a problem giving me what I needed—that is, company support for Okey Justice. At some point, I made things clearer for them.

"You fellows want everything I've got," I said. "But you're out there helping Ray Watts for sheriff! Well, Ray Watts is a dead dodo bird. He can't win. I've got the election officers. And, like it or not, I've got the United Mine Workers with me."

I reminded them that, outside of Okey, the company favored almost all the other candidates on my slate.

"Now I'm gonna be as hard politically with you as you are with your men," I said. "I've got a tough row to hoe. I've *got* to have your support in the sheriff's race if I'm going to win these others and support your man as president."

We left there that day with a new understanding. I would work for Kennedy, and they would spread the good word about my candidates to their people. Not long after that meeting, I had proof the company was living up to its end of the bargain. I ran into an Island Creek superintendent who told me he'd been called into the office that day. He said the company executives had been "talking up" Okey Justice for sheriff.

"By God, this election is changing, ain't it, Raymond?" he said.

"It sure looks that way," I commented.

With Island Creek behind us, my power grew bigger than ever before. It helped me spread out beyond Logan County. I could start things up with friends and other politicians in other southern West Virginia counties—Mingo, Wyoming, and McDowell, for example. Island Creek employed more than a thousand people in Logan County and a little more than that in Wyoming and McDowell. They employed some 1,200 in Mingo. Wherever the company had a mine in these counties, I could go to the politicians I knew there.

"You get with us on Kennedy," I said, "and I can help you line up Island Creek for the people you want."

One of these county leaders might ask me for something—a favor for a mine worker or a superintendent he needed in his campaign. I put them in touch with the right company officials, some of whom were new to the area and hadn't learned their way around yet. All I had to do was call my contact high up in Island Creek, and the favor was done. In return, the county politicians in the southern part of the state all turned their support to John F. Kennedy. I was hittin' licks for Kennedy and hittin' licks for local politicians too. Before long, all these counties were lined up for Kennedy—and nobody knew a damn thing about it.[2]

A day or so after the meeting at Island Creek, I was telling my friends I was ready to take a break, that I was going south for a couple of days. Actually, Jim McCahey had me flown out of Logan County—to Baltimore, I believe—to discuss Kennedy's West Virginia campaign with some people he knew there.

I was met at the other end by a limousine which took me to a hotel, where I sat in an upstairs lounge with five or six other men. I delivered the same message to them I'd given all along. I'm not even sure who I was talking to that day, but I talked to them just like I do anybody else.

"Boys," I said, "You're goin' at it all wrong in West Virginia. You're gettin' took down there, and you'll lose it all if you ain't careful. These fellows you're getting with ain't the ones you want to be working on. He has to get in better with the *real* politicians."

---

2. The most powerful machines in some of these counties may already have been "lined-up" with the Kennedy campaign. In at least one case, Raymond seems to have been dealing with the competing "underdog" faction. (It was part of the Kennedy campaign's strategy to build up whatever faction favored its candidate.) In the case of Logan and other southern counties, the result was to swamp the field with support for JFK.—T. S.

I told them that too many local boys were pulling them for their money. I agreed to work for them, and they agreed to put something into our organization.

Now, political organizations do cost money. If you ever get yourself one together, you're going to need it. All the candidates on my slate donated to the campaign, and Kennedy was no different. Some people might suggest that Raymond Chafin took money for himself. Let them. It ain't true. If it was, I wouldn't be writing this. All anyone has to do is come see where Louise and I live right now. I like it, it's not bad. But it sure isn't the home of a man who got rich off of politics. I could have gotten something for myself, but I never was a "money man." The game was always the same for me: winning at politics.

At this Baltimore meeting, these men asked what it cost me to run a campaign in Logan County. Back then, it took about $100,000, gathered mostly from the candidates and interest groups like the coal companies.[3] The money was spent, in part, to hire car drivers and workers at the polls on election day. And—there's no point in denying it now—to buy votes. I'm not just talking about cash exchanges, although that happened too. Just as often we'd pay for a driver's license for someone who couldn't afford it, or an electric bill, or something like that.

Of course the main tool we had for telling everyone where we stood was the slates—the cards with all our candidates' names on them and my name at the bottom. These fellows in that hotel lounge became real interested in the slates, and I showed them a sample of the ones we'd already printed. Hubert Humphrey's name was on top. They passed those cards around and looked at them. One fellow asked me what it would take to take Humphrey's name off the slate and get John Kennedy's name on. He was asking for a dollar figure.

---

3. There were no limits on campaign contributions in 1960.—T. S.

I'd already gotten most of the campaign set up, and I didn't need much, so I decided to keep the figure real small—just four digits—a little more than what my local candidates donated.

"About thirty-five," I said, meaning $3,500.

"That's no problem," these fellows replied. "We'll take care of that. . . . No problem."

They agreed to have a whole new batch of slates printed up in New York with Kennedy's name on them.[4]

The night after I came home from that trip, Elvie Curry called me. It was two o'clock in the morning.

"You asleep?" he asked.

"Hell yeah, I'm asleep!"

I figured he'd been drinking or something.

"Well, I don't care," said Elvie. "I'm comin' up."

"What's goin' on?"

"I'll tell you when I get there."

It didn't take him long to get up to Cow Creek. We sat down in my living room, upstairs from the Blankenship Grocery.

"Raymond," he said, "We're gonna have to do something about this Kennedy thing. We're gonna lose this election the way things are going now!"

Elvie laid it all out for me.

"Kennedy's gaining ground in Chapmanville and our boys are all wrong," he said. "Our candidates are wrong and they're all gonna get beat. You have to do something!"

I'd been dying for someone to tell me that. Our candidates—Judge Chambers and Okey Justice, especially—were out there

---

4. In his book, *Kennedy vs. Humphrey, West Virginia 1960*, Dan B. Fleming, Jr., quotes Sargent Shriver as saying he "vividly" recalled a "private meeting with a top Logan County official a few days before the May 10 voting and being able to persuade the leader to switch from Humphrey to Kennedy." When Fleming asked Shriver how he was able to accomplish this, Shriver reportedly laughed and said, "I'm a lawyer and I don't know."—T. S.

blasting away at Kennedy. He was getting popular, though, so our people were turning a lot of folks against themselves. I could imagine Ray Watts and Claude Ellis really having themselves a laugh over that situation.

I'd known all along that we had to do something about it, but I didn't know what. Even hearing Elvie say it, I didn't know—and election day was about a week away. I told Elvie to go home and get some sleep.

"We'll have a meeting in the morning," I said.

The next day, I called my core group into our room at the Aracoma Hotel.

"We're gonna have to be careful," I told them. "Take it easy on this presidential thing. Don't talk about it. Just tread water."

Bus Perry spoke up. "It's up to you, Raymond," he said. "You're the boss. Whatever you say, we'll do."

Later, I talked to each of our four main candidates—Judge Chambers, Oval Damron, Okey Justice, and Glenn Jackson. I met with them one at a time.

"You *have* to stay out of this presidential race," I insisted. "People *know* we're for Humphrey. We've got his signs up and his literature out. Just *stay out of it* and be for the rest of your county ticket!"

Some of them didn't like hearing that, especially Judge Chambers. Ray Watts had been working on him, blowing smoke up his ass and bad-mouthing our other candidates to him.

"Goddammit," said the judge, "I can't keep quiet and be for all these other son-of-a-bitches you're for!"

I sat down with him. I had to be honest with him. "Judge, I hate to tell you this," I said, "but you're not popular! You've sent a lot of people to jail and they don't especially like you for it. You're popular with the better class of people, but there's not enough of them in this county to elect you! Practically nobody

THE 1960 ELECTION

over in Harts Creek likes you. If you ain't careful, you'll end up settin' and rockin' on your own front porch, while the other fellow down the street wears that black robe of yours!"

As hot-tempered as he was, Cush Chambers—and all the rest of them, too—understood what I was saying. No candidate wants to lose an election. So, for the most part, they kept quiet after that. (If there was any exception, it was Okey Justice. He kept going strong for Humphrey right up to election day, and it almost got him beat.)

During this time, the last week of the campaign, the race had really grown hot; Humphrey and Kennedy were knocking away at each other and the whole state was turned upside down. The candidates had a live debate on TV, and all kinds of local and national news reporters were running around, trying to figure out who would come out on top.[5]

Local candidates, of course, didn't use television back then—they used loudspeakers. We mounted them on the tops of cars and sent people around, talking into that microphone and blasting our candidates' names across every hill and holler.

Lonnie Nelson did this for us. He was an independent man and a strapping big fellow who would fight you in a minute. But he was a Free-Will Baptist preacher and he spoke well, so we put him in one of those loudspeaker cars.

Lonnie didn't like the Kennedys at all, though. He was strictly against them, a strong Humphrey man. One day in May, he was driving around in Superior Bottom, a black community, talking about our candidates. Then, he decided to fire away at John F. Kennedy. John-Kennedy-this and Kennedy-that.

---

5. Remarkably, while many of the seasoned politicians could see the writing on the wall, most of the national and local press were predicting a Humphrey win.—T. S.

Everybody in Superior Bottom knew my phone number at the Aracoma, and they called in just as fast as we could pick up the telephone—telling me how Lonnie Nelson was hurting my candidates up there.

"You'd better get that preacher off that thing!" they said. "He's up here cussin' Kennedy!"

Right away, I phoned the sheriff's office and told Sheriff "Uncle Ed" McDonald to have his deputies hunt Lonnie Nelson down. I told him I wanted them to get Lonnie off that loudspeaker and bring him in to me.

"And I don't mean in thirty minutes!" I said. "I mean *now!*"

I was furious—Curry mad. The deputies brought Lonnie in there and I jumped all over him.

"What the hell are you doin' out there?" I yelled. "I've got you out there to run *our* candidates! Goddammit, we ain't running for president! Don't you go over to Superior Bottom no more! And stay out of the goddamn presidential election!"

I was cussing and raising so much hell my secretary had to come in and calm me down. To his credit, Lonnie never got a bit mad at me. He said he was sorry, that he'd just gotten carried away.

By the last week of the election, I was getting it from all sides. Politicians from other parts of the state were coming in, working to split me and my faction. Wally Barron, the leading gubernatorial candidate, and some of his people came to me. They wanted to know why I didn't come out for Kennedy. My sense was that Barron didn't give a damn who won the presidential race, and they didn't care about me and my faction either. I figured they'd been betting on Ray Watts and were helping him needle me a little, maybe to get me in trouble with my own. I told Barron I'd sent Humphrey's money back.

"I'm not in this presidential thing," I said. "I'm staying the hell out of it."

Not long after that, Kennedy spoke in Charleston and Louise and Margaret went to hear him again. Once more, Claude Ellis spotted them in the crowd, their fingers curled through the chain-link fence at the airport.

Remembering what had happened in Omar, Claude saw his chance to embarrass me another time. He leaned over to some of Kennedy's people and told them to bring Louise and Margaret right up to the plane. They took them up there and they met Kennedy right as he came down the steps. There were the photographers, going to work again.

Claude did it, I figure, to cause me trouble back in Logan. Of course, he didn't know that I'd already gotten with Kennedy, so those pictures really didn't hurt me at all. In fact, they helped me. When I got ready to jump ship, everybody could say they'd seen it coming all along.

By the end of the campaign, the whole Kennedy family had gotten involved in West Virginia and several of them had visited Logan. JFK's sister, Eunice Shriver, both his brothers, and even his mother stayed a night or two at the Aracoma. Rose Kennedy helped plan several events for the county women, and she didn't hold back on the supplies, either. One day, I decided I wanted to meet Senator Kennedy's mother, so I slipped over to one of her rooms at the Aracoma. She was giving orders—sending for a case of coffee—when we were introduced.

"Are you going to help my son win this election?" she asked me.

I just smiled at her and put my finger to my lips.

A few days before election day, someone called from the Kennedy headquarters in Charleston and told me I should meet a plane coming into Taplan Airport that afternoon. They suggested I have a couple of bodyguards with me because they were sending us a little "something to work with."

I never did need a bodyguard for myself, but I went to Bus Perry and told him, "You're my man, Bus. I want you to get ready."

He didn't know exactly what was going on, but he was glad to go. It was pouring rain that day, and we bought the best umbrella we could find. I made sure that Bus got himself a good raincoat, and I took him back to my office. I gave him a little handgun I had and told him to put it in his pocket.

"God," he said. "I ain't never carried no gun before!"

"Just put it in your damned pocket!" I said.

We took his Cadillac through the rain, up to Taplan, just outside Logan. We walked across the swinging bridge to get to the edge of the runway, where we waited together under a hangar.

A small plane came into sight, but it didn't land for a while; it just circled around.

"Damn, Raymond, that fellow's lost!" said Bus.

"He'll land."

The plane came down and we started out there.

"Come on," I said. "They have some campaign literature for us."

Robert McDonough, an industrialist from Parkersburg, had been running Kennedy's entire show in West Virginia. He'd gotten with them early on, and I'd talked with him a couple of other times. He was in that plane with two other men. When it landed, McDonough and one of the others climbed out and handed me two briefcases.

I asked what was in them.

"I don't know," McDonough shrugged. "It's from headquarters."

We thanked them and put the cases in the trunk of our car. Bus had noticed the heavy seals on those cases and he knew right away what was in there.

"Boy," he smiled. "This must be some kind of special literature!"

He didn't know how much cash was in those cases and, to tell you the truth, neither did I. I told Bus to get his list of precincts ready; that we'd be refiguring some of the money we'd be paying our workers.

Bus dropped me off downtown, quickly returning the gun. We locked those briefcases in my station wagon. When I went up to room 220, Elvie Curry was there.

"Hey Elvie," I said. "Let's you and me take a ride up to Cow Creek."

At my place, we cut away the seals, opened those cases, and saw all that money—separated into packages of fives, tens, and twenty-dollar bills.

"Oh my God, Elvie," I said. "We sure got everything we need now!"

But the more I looked, the more I knew that someone in Kennedy's outfit had misunderstood me. I realized then that those men in Baltimore came from a whole different world than I did. They spoke a different language. I'd said one thing, but they'd heard something else—a much bigger figure. I'd said "thirty-five," talking in hundreds; they'd heard thousands. There was thirty-five thousand dollars in those cases—plus more money for some of my contacts in the other counties. I got on the phone to Jim McCahey.

"I believe they made a mistake!" I said. "They sent more than I told them to!"

"Hell, no!" McCahey said. "There's no mistake! We know you're doing your job!"

I still think that I was the only one around here who ever told them the truth—even if it was kind of an accident. It would have been the easiest thing in the world for me to keep some of that money. But I spent it all, just the way they wanted me to. I spent it all on that election. . . . But I'm getting ahead of things.

Elvie and I resealed those cases and took them down to his mother's house. She was an old widow, living in a little place on the Left Fork of Cow Creek. We told her it was campaign literature and asked her to keep it under a bed until we got back, sometime before election day.

Bus got his list out, and we just doubled or tripled the amounts we were putting into each precinct. There was so much cash, we could even hire some of Ray Watts's best workers and precinct captains away from him.

Meanwhile, I called the political leaders I'd been dealing with in some of these other southern counties. By that time, they were more than willing to put Kennedy on their slates. Many of them had been supporting Hubert Humphrey, but he'd never come through with anything. It was almost like he'd given up in southern West Virginia.

As election day came closer, I got less and less sleep. I had the toughest time in the world keeping everything organized, choosing election officers while keeping a tight lid on everything. Kennedy's people were demanding my attention, sometimes calling me at four or five o'clock in the morning. I didn't mind working with them but, with all the other things going on, it began to wear on me.

My political enemies were busy too. I don't know who it was, but I think one of them was probably behind a little surprise that was waiting for me one night near the Aracoma. I was on my way to our headquarters with about eight thousand dollars in campaign money in my pocket. I was right across the street from the Harris Funeral Home when two men came out of the alley ahead of me. One of them was holding a heavy piece of mine cable.

That was enough for me. I'd always been a good student of "George Steele's School of Politics," so I still carried my little snub-nosed .38 on me. I didn't think twice about pulling it out and firing a couple shots at those two fellows. Apparently, they hadn't bargained on that, and they took off across the street. It didn't take long for two policemen to show up.

"What's going on, Raymond? What were those shots?"

Now, the city of Logan was still run by Republicans in those days, and most of them were on Ray Watts's side. The chief of police was close friends with Claude Ellis. They wouldn't have cared a hoot about what happened to Raymond Chafin if they'd caught him with an illegal pistol and eight thousand dollars in his pockets.

"Hell, boys," I told them. "Wasn't nothing but an old car going through here! Just a backfire."

But the incident only added to the weight of the election on me. My friends started noticing that something was distracting me. They didn't know it was the Kennedy campaign. My people started getting angry, saying I wasn't doing enough for their races. With all the pressure, I decided it was time to tell my closest friends that we would be supporting Kennedy. It was Friday, May 6, four days before election day. Elvie was the first to come in and see me.

"Elvie," I said, "I've decided I've got to be for Kennedy."

He gave a long, low whistle. "What are we gonna do about the judge?" he asked. "What about the prosecutor and the sheriff?"

"I'll line 'em up," I said, "when the time comes for it."

Then we told Bus, who wasn't surprised. By this time he'd seen the writing on the wall, and he was real relieved to hear the news. "That's the best damned move you've ever made," he grinned.

"Well," I said. "I guess your boy showed us after all."

The next day, Saturday—three days before the election—Morgan Massey had a dinner at the Holden Field House. He was calling it a "delayed Christmas dinner" for all his supervisors and other employees from around the state. I hadn't gone, but apparently people started asking about me, so they called me over there. Morgan made a special effort to come over and shake my hand and we talked. He asked whether I'd thought any more about throwing my support behind Jack Kennedy.

"Yeah," I told him. "I sure have."

"It would look awful bad for me—you working for me and all—if he lost in Logan County," Morgan said.

"He hasn't lost it yet, has he?"

"No."

"Well," I grinned. "Just go hide yourself someplace and watch it, big boy!"

The next day, Sunday, some other local coal executives decided to have a big breakfast meeting with some of my candidates, whose campaigns they'd helped finance. This was at a company lodge up in Chauncey Hollow. My candidates were all there, along with several coal operators, and Jim McCahey was there. We'd decided it would be good to have all these big guns around when I told Judge Chambers and my other anti-Kennedy candidates that I was throwing my support behind the senator from Massachusetts.

We got up there and had our breakfast. People talked about the election, including the presidential race. Judge Chambers immediately started in on Kennedy.

"By God, there's no way he can win! . . ." The same old tune. The judge became real hot about it. The more I listened, the more I decided to hold off from telling anyone what I was up to. I sat there and kept my mouth shut. The breakfast broke up and, outside, McCahey walked up beside me.

"Damn!" he said. "You didn't even *mention* Kennedy in there!"

By this time, I was so goddamned tired of the whole thing—everybody coming around to see what I was doing for them. I lost my temper.

"Goddammit, Jim, you just leave this damned election to me! I'll handle it! You don't know anything about Logan County politics and, by God, you're going to get me in trouble! It wasn't the *time* for me to mention Kennedy in there!"

I left with Bus, who drove his old Cadillac down the hill. Judge Chambers rode in the front seat.

We came around the hollow and approached a place where a local congregation was holding a big Sunday baptism in the creek. That crowd was big enough to block the road, so Bus stopped the car and decided to have a little fun with the judge.

"Come on, Raymond," he said. "Let's you and me get out and pray with them! Come on, judge, we'll get them to baptize you—make a Catholic out of you!"

Goddamn! I thought Cush Chambers would go right through the roof of that car! He didn't like that kidding—from Bus or anybody. The judge liked to come off as being dignified, and he knew how to raise hell.

". . . By God," he said, "You boys will see what happens with this thing, come Tuesday!"

Down the road a ways, after he'd calmed down a bit, Judge Chambers turned to Bus and said, "Doggone it, Bus, *you're* not for Kennedy are you?"

Bus told him about his son and all the young people being for JFK.

"By God, I'll tell you one thing," Chambers said. "I ain't never gonna be for no Kennedy!"

This was my chance to do a little preachin' of my own.

"Well, you'd do best to keep your mouth shut about it," I said. "You're running for judge, not president, and you'd better be careful! . . . I've got all the respect in the world for you, Judge, and I'm married to your cousin! But you know you shouldn't be talking that way. Just let me and Bus handle it." I'd said it that way to pump up Bus some.

The "final showdown" with the judge, Oval Damron, Okey Justice, Glenn Jackson, and the others didn't come until the next day, Monday, May 9—the day before election day. We were right up to the election, and I'd kept everything to myself. I couldn't believe that word hadn't gotten out yet about what I'd been doing.

It was about ten o'clock Monday morning when I called everybody in—all my major candidates and all my main leaders. We gathered in our little room at the Aracoma, with election workers and everybody spilling out into the hall. They all came to hear what I had to say. I just stretched myself out on that bed in room 220 and folded my hands behind my head. All four of them—Judge Chambers, Oval Damron, Okey Justice, and Glenn Jackson—were up front, right at the foot of the bed. Everything was set up, and it was too late for any of them to do anything about it.

"Boys," I said. "The time has come when I've got to make a decision. I don't care whether you like it or not; this is the way it's gonna be...."

I looked hard at Judge Chambers.

"Judge, we're gonna have a hard enough time electing you, even with things the way they are. And you can go out of here hollerin' and cussin' however much you want, but you know damned well that I'm for you one hundred percent. And every one of these fellers sittin' around here—Bus Perry, Elvie Curry, Arnold Harkins, and all the rest—they're all for you. We got just about every precinct in this county set to be for you tomorrow....

"But I have got to make a change, and it's for *your* benefit. If I don't, I figure you'll get beat by one or two thousand votes. I'm telling all you candidates: Kennedy's got to come! Or I've got to go!"

It was like a lightening bolt went through that room when I said that. Those men argued and fussed, and it sounded like hell. But it was too late—and I wasn't having any of it, besides.

"By God," I told them. "The slates are all made up, and I have them right here! We got all the money we need, and if somebody don't want to be with us on this thing, then he can just go home and stay off the damned streets!

"But we have *got* to be with Kennedy tomorrow, and that's the way it's gonna be! Now, I want everyone to get a pocketful of these slates and get them out to people! Hell, we've all got work to do.... That's it!"

The judge and a couple of others stomped out of there, but there was nothing they could do. There was nothing anyone could do, not Ray Watts or Claude Ellis or anyone. The rest of them said they were with me. They all took some slates—printed in New York City with Kennedy's name right on the top. They went off to do what they had to, spreading those slates to all the precincts. We got some JFK posters and went all over the place, taking down Humphrey's signs and putting up Kennedy's.

That night, I went to McDowell, Wyoming, Mingo, and Boone counties. I carried the Kennedy campaign money for their organizations to pay their election day workers. I told them all pretty much the same thing.

"Boys," I said, "You'd better bring him."

And they brought him. People are still trying to figure out how John F. Kennedy did so well in southern West Virginia, heart of the "anti-Catholic" Bible belt. McDowell County gave him 84 percent of the vote, the highest in the state. The second highest was Wyoming County, with 78 percent. Logan and Mingo each delivered more than 55 percent for Kennedy, and he carried the entire state by more than 84,000 votes.

The results of the West Virginia primary caused Hubert Humphrey to drop out of the race the next day. Later that summer, the Democrats at the national convention were solidly behind one man: John F. Kennedy for president.

After he was elected, his people offered me just about any kind of job I wanted. I told them I didn't want anything. We got some money for a new courthouse here in Logan, and we got part of a dam out of it. But I never really asked them for anything. Never cared to.

Ray Watts and Claude Ellis, naturally, were real sore about the results of that election. I believe they had something to do with the special grand jury that was called to look into some of the "excesses" that went on out in the precincts.[6] I don't remember how many people they indicted, but they had a special judge come in to hear it.

He called all of us into his office—all the faction leaders—and chewed us out, telling us it was all just a bunch of politics. He told us that one side was just as guilty as the other, and he threw the whole thing out of court.

We left that judge's office—Ray Watts and his crowd and everybody from my crowd—and we all had breakfast together. A couple of years after that, I helped Ray and Claude get themselves a couple of nice state jobs.

---

6. One day after the election, the *Logan County Banner* described the election as a Bacchanalia of "flagrant vote-buying, whiskey flowing like water, and coercion of voters.... You name it," said the paper, "and we just about had it."—T. S.

11 White House Emissary

KENNEDY'S PEOPLE CALLED ME SEVERAL times after he became president. The first call came in January 1961, right after he took office. Once he'd won the primary here, he didn't need to come back for the general. He knew he could count on this state against Nixon.

It was on a Sunday, about ten o'clock in the morning, when the woman called me.

"Mr. Raymond Chafin?"

"Yes, ma'am."

"The president would like to see you."

Now, it had been several months since I dealt with John Kennedy or any of his people, and this was a voice I'd never heard before. I figured it was someone pulling my leg.

"Oh no," I said. "I'll need a little time to study on that."

She was real nice, though, and she agreed to call back in an hour or so. I hung up the phone and started talking to Louise about it.

"Well," she said. "You almost act like you believe it."

"I just don't know . . . maybe it was them. If that lady wasn't from Washington, someone sure did a good job of faking it."

I got to thinking about going to the White House. I'd been to Washington before, of course—several times—but I'd sure never been asked to see the president.

"Hell," I said. "What would they want me up there for?"

Louise suggested I call Bus.

Now, as I've said, Bus Perry was a smart man. But when I told him about that phone call, he got real excited.

"I'll be right over!" he said, and he was.

"They're gonna call you back?" he asked.

"In about an hour or so."

"God, Raymond, you've got to go!" said Bus. "I don't hardly know a *governor* in West Virginia who's ever been asked to see the president!"

Kennedy's secretary did call us back (it wasn't a hoax), and she asked me when I could be in Washington.

"You tell me when," I said, "and I'll be there."

She set me up a date, and Bus offered to drive me in his Cadillac. By the time the big day arrived, I'd bought myself a brand-new suit. We came up through Charleston, where we stayed overnight, and drove into Washington the next evening. We checked into the Mayflower Hotel, where Kennedy's people had made reservations for us. The next morning, we took a cab to the White House. But, try as I did, they wouldn't let Bus in to see the president.

They showed me into a big reception room with beautiful paintings on the walls. I waited there for about fifteen minutes, and I'd never been so nervous in all my life. I was shaking so much I wondered whether I was going to be able to talk at all. It was like getting ready to make a big political speech. I'd never been speechless before, but I'd seen people get that way. They'd get up before the crowds and just couldn't think. They froze up, couldn't say a word.

"By God, Raymond, you can't stop now," I told myself. "You can't freeze up now. You've got to get in there and talk to the president—answer his questions."

My mind turned to home, to Cow Creek and all the people I knew there. I thought of my Grandma Curry, back when I was just a kid, when she rode with me on the back of her horse. I smiled to myself and wished Grandma Mary could see me now. Wouldn't she be proud! Her own grandson, called to the White House by the president of the United States. And me, with just a seventh-grade education. I thought of all my people on Cow Creek, how they'd helped me through my life. I remembered all the hard times and hard work I'd shared with them.

I was feeling better by the time I was shown into John Kennedy's office. He came around from behind his desk to shake my hand. We took chairs in front of the desk; he had a rocker that he pulled up right across from mine. Then a secretary came in with a clipboard and told him he had ten minutes to spend with me. The president looked up at her and said something that really made me feel good.

"I called this man in to see me," he said. "He has all the time he needs."

I was there a full hour.

Kennedy opened by making it clear that he still wanted to do something for the people of West Virginia. He had seen it all pretty much the way it was. The coal industry was in a slump, and things were pretty bad for a lot of folks in our part of the world; for some, it was as bad as it had been during the Hoover panic. There were hundreds of miners out of work—and that was just around Omar, not even counting the other towns along Island Creek. Unemployment compensation had run out for a lot of folks, and they had nothing coming in at all. A lot of families didn't have welfare, and there were the older miners, sick with black lung—what we called "miner's asthma." There was no hospitalization for a lot of them.[1] No nothing.

Kennedy talked about the people in these counties who were on relief, and he told me a little about the programs he was starting up. His first order as president had been to increase the amount of government commodities people were getting.[2] For some, this government-surplus food—unbleached flour, yellow cornmeal, rice, butter, oats, and lard—was about the only food they had to live on. People who weren't working helped to give it out.

But I knew a little something about the commodities program in Logan County. I knew plenty of people who'd been on relief; I'd been on it myself. Raising the variety and amount of commodity food really didn't impress me, and I had to tell the president as much.

"Truthfully, I don't see how it's going to help," I said. "People don't eat the commodities they're getting now. They don't like that government food. They take it home and give it to whatever hogs and chickens they have."

Kennedy argued that people would have a better variety of food available once his program was in place.

1. Sometime in 1963 Kennedy came to Wheeling, and I was one of a few people who got to meet with him there. I wanted to ask him about our new county courthouse, and while I was talking with him, Kennedy said he was still thinking about the miners of southern West Virginia. "You can go back and tell people that we're going to do something about it," he said.

He was talking about black lung, and he was true to his word. The Kennedy administration started the first federal black-lung program.

2. Meyer Feldman, deputy special counsel to the president, recalls that Kennedy directed him to draw up Executive Order No. 1, raising the commodity levels, within hours of the 1961 inauguration—before the president had spent a full day in office.—T. S.

"That doesn't matter," I said. "People don't want it. People are tired of the commodities. They just don't like them. Honestly, I don't think your improvements are going to help people any. What they want most is a job."

Now, I could tell that he didn't especially like hearing all this from me. I think he was even a little stunned at my reaction. But there was nothing I could do about it. He'd asked me what I thought, and I'd told him. Hell, I figured that's why I was there.

Jack Kennedy might not have liked hearing everything you had to say to him, but he still wanted to hear it. This was another reason he impressed me so much as a politician. He knew I didn't agree with everything he was doing, but he didn't care. He encouraged me to talk because he realized that I knew what I was talking about, and he wanted to hear it. He *needed* to hear it.

"I've been on relief, Mr. President," I told him. "So I know how it is. In the old days, under Roosevelt, my mother got a grocery order that she could use in a real grocery store."

I told him about taking that grocery order down to U. G. Browning's store and getting whatever food our family needed. Kennedy listened for a while, asking some questions. Then, he buzzed his secretary, she came in, and he told her he wanted to see several other people right away. They must have been right close by because it didn't take long for four or five men and one woman to get there.[3]

He introduced me to those people and told them what I'd been saying. He had me go into it again about the food-order

---

3. Raymond doesn't remember the names of any of these people. Theodore Sorensen and Meyer Feldman say that while the meeting may well have occurred, they have no recollection of it. Officials do say, however, that the woman in the meeting was likely Assistant Secretary of Labor Esther Peterson. Peterson also does not recall this specific meeting but says that it is very possible that she was in the room.—T. S.

program under Roosevelt. I was less nervous by this time and, as I was talking, they started asking me questions. At some point, I believe I offered up my old idea of doing away with the commodities altogether.

"Mr. President, you ought to just get rid of them," I said. "People would rather starve than eat that flour or cornmeal. The kids don't like the powdered milk, and they won't drink it. People don't have a way of getting meat, sugar, or the other things they need, and they just can't get along the way things are now. You've got to fix them up with a job or something, or give them a check or money or something else they can use to buy the things they need at a store."

One of Kennedy's people spoke up. This fellow had a white collar, just as stiff around his neck as a horse's collar.

"Mr. President," he said. "If you stop the commodities, you're going to hurt yourself with the farmers."

The woman disagreed. "If you give people money—or something they can use to buy food," she said, "they'll be buying the farmers' product."

There was more talk on the subject. Kennedy agreed that government-surplus food, alone, wasn't doing the job he wanted. He said he was concerned about people who were sick and couldn't get by on it. My impression was that this group was supposed to come up with a plan for people on relief.[4] Before I left, John Kennedy told me to expect another call.

"This is not the end of this," he said. "I'd appreciate it if you could come back again."

"Mr. President," I said, "I'd be honored."

Bus and I drove back to Logan, and within a few weeks, the West Virginia Department of Welfare was busy organizing a fed-

---

4. The food-stamp program likely had already been under consideration by Kennedy staffers. The program was announced on February 1, 1961.—T. S.

eral experiment. The first food stamps were handed out in McDowell County that spring.

Sometime after that, the president called me back to Washington. He told me he wanted me to travel around in McDowell to see how things were going with the food-stamp program. Specifically, he wanted me to talk to people, especially the local merchants, to see how they liked trading in food stamps. He asked me what I would need to do the job, and I told him I wouldn't need anything. I came back to West Virginia, drove to McDowell County, and started looking around.

I hadn't realized it before, but McDowell County had been hard-hit by the economic situation, even before people in some of these other places were hurting very much. People there had always been real dependent on the coal industry. When the mines shut down, almost everything else shut down too.

Some of these coal companies, for example, had been supplying electricity and water to people's houses. Even in 1961, some of the companies still owned the houses, and they ran people's power through their lines, charging the miners for utilities every month—when they were working, that is. When the mines shut down, the companies just pulled the plug. They cut off people's power and water. You'd see folks lined up at the hillside springs to get water. Some of them walked three and four miles just to get their drinking water. Imagine that: no water running in the house—no bath water, no kitchen water. You carried in what you got. To me, McDowell seemed to be the worst off, but I knew the same thing was happening all over southern West Virginia.

I chose not to meet with any politicians or anybody like that. I was asked to talk to the merchants, and that's what I was going to do. I took my friend Orin Beaufort with me because Orin had delivered soda pop to just about every store in McDowell

County. He knew all the store owners. We spent two days traveling around, just talking to people, asking them what they thought of Kennedy and the new food-stamp program.

A week or two after I got back to Logan, I returned to Washington to make my report. Most of the merchants were pleased with the food stamps. We ran into two or three fellows who were sour about it, but they still accepted them. My impression was that these fellows just didn't want to change—or they still didn't like Kennedy. But there was really no problem with the new program in McDowell, and I was glad to be able to give it a positive report in Washington.

By the fall of 1964, food stamps were being handed out to more than 350,000 people in West Virginia and forty-two other states. Of course, by that time, John Kennedy was gone. The president's assassination was an especially hard blow to this state. His successful campaign here and the programs he initiated made him special to West Virginia and its people.

I was driving to Charleston for a meeting with the governor when I heard about it. I got the news from a toll-taker on the West Virginia Turnpike. By the time I got into Charleston, the entire state capitol had been shut down. Everybody had gone home to learn more about what was going on in Dallas. Out on the capitol lawn, I remember, several people were wiping tears from their eyes. They had good reason. With John F. Kennedy's death, West Virginians lost just about the best friend they ever had.

12 1964–1984: Moore and Rockefeller

IN 1964, JACK FERRELL, THE MAN WE'D SIGNED on as our faction's treasurer, wanted to be Logan County's sheriff. Jack's wife had been serving on the Democratic Executive Committee. She had always voted with me—helping me stay in as chairman—and I'd gotten along well enough with Jack, so I decided to help him get in as sheriff. We had to force some of the others to accept the idea, but we did it. We got Jack elected.

As soon he got in there, though, Jack started doing a lot of things he shouldn't have been doing. He fell out with me and ignored everything that anybody ever told him. I had to remind him that he needed to keep all his friends around him, but Jack wouldn't listen.

"All I need with me is six," he said.

"What does that mean?" I asked.

"All I need is six friends to be my pallbearers."

A man is bound to get into trouble with an attitude like that, and it didn't take long with Jack Ferrell. He got into the bridge-construction business while he was sheriff, which was against the law at that time, so the County Commission impeached him sometime after the 1964 election. In the meantime, though, Jack had started up a whole new faction, made up of people who had fallen out with me. And, even though he had lost the sheriff's job, Jack got me voted out as chairman, basically taking the executive committee away from me.

Jack appealed his impeachment and a judge held things up for some time before ruling on it. When the ruling came out against Jack, the County Commission had to appoint someone else as sheriff.

I don't know why but, at that point, it seemed like everybody in the world wanted to be sheriff. Earl Tomblin, Alvis Porter, Joe Blair, and Okey Hager were all in the running. There were even some other characters around who were trying to bribe people—trying to buy their way into the office.

I never did understand why everybody in Logan County wanted to be sheriff. George Steele and I were about the only ones around who didn't want it. George used to tell me, "Raymond, don't ever get yourself elected sheriff. You can only be in it for one term, and it'll kill you politically, with all the fighting and squabbling you have to get into. It's just a dead-end job."

Being sheriff wasn't just bad for me politically; it wasn't good for me financially, either. Some people made money being sheriff—and in politics, generally—but I always had a good outside job, so I never needed politics for that. The County Commission asked me if I wanted to be sheriff, but I turned it down.

Time was short; the commission had to vote on the sheriff's appointment in just a day or two. We needed a good sheriff, and I decided to see if I could start putting something together for one of our school board members, Bill Abraham.

I called one of the commissioners, Bill Dingess, who was in Kentucky at the time. He owned a big electrical-contracting firm and had been with Jack Ferrell's bunch, but they'd had some kind of a falling-out. So I called Bill Dingess to sound him out on Bill Abraham. I hadn't mentioned any names before Bill Dingess said something that really threw me for a loop.

"I'd kind of like to be sheriff," he said.

I was quiet for a minute. "Bill, are you sure you can be sheriff with your company and all?"

"Hell," he said, "I'd sell my company if I could be sheriff!"

I couldn't fight it. The commission voted Bill Dingess in, but the day after they voted, Bill announced he had to give it up. His lawyers had told him he'd be *crazy* to sell all his holdings to be the Logan County sheriff. I called a meeting at my house and invited Bill Dingess, along with Red Bivens—both of them county commissioners.

There were a lot of deals made at my home on Cow Creek. It was a safe place. Whenever I had something really important to discuss, I told people to "meet me under the rock cliff." That was friendly talk for an invitation to my house, which was built right in front of one.

After Bill Dingess resigned, about eight of us met at my house. Even before the meeting, though, I'd started trying to line people up for Bill Abraham. My feeling was that, after Jack's impeachment, we needed a man whose reputation stood beyond reproach.

"Gentlemen," I said, "Bill here says he can't be sheriff. We're going to have to pick another one. I want you boys to listen to me a minute and try to decide on some things. I've talked to a couple of you already, and I don't mean to run around you on this, but you know we need to do the right thing here.

"The fact is that we're in trouble. This thing with the impeachment could make us lose this county. You know how many people have been trying to come in and buy their way in as sheriff. But, as far as I'm concerned, the job is *not for sale*.

We're gonna to have to put somebody in there who can win the next election."

I brought up Bill Abraham's name at that point. Red Bivens and Bill, who were two-thirds of the County Commission, immediately said they would be behind him. But some of the others in my group frowned on it. (I don't think Bus Perry liked it too much, for example. Bus liked having Bill Abraham on the school board.) But the commissioners put Bill in as the interim sheriff, and that's when all the fun started.

Bill became sheriff, and we figured he'd make a good candidate in the 1966 election running for Jack Ferrell's unexpired term. We needed the Democratic Executive Committee to support putting Bill's name on the ballot, but Jack Ferrell still controlled the committee, and they refused to put Bill on the ticket. No matter what I did or said, Jack's people just wouldn't do it.

Instead, the Democrats did something that made no sense at all. They made Jack's daddy the 1966 candidate for sheriff. Now, there was nothing wrong with J. W. Ferrell, Sr., although he was an old man by that time. It just didn't look good—him coming in as sheriff after his son had just been impeached. It was too obvious, and it irritated people.

The next thing I did you might call "sneaky," but I call it damned good politics. The Republicans didn't have anyone to run for sheriff that year. I had a good friend, Lloyd Brumfield, who was on the Republican Executive Committee. Lloyd knew more politics and was a lot easier to get along with than most Republicans. (Some of them wouldn't even speak to a Democrat unless they had to.) So, I ran into Lloyd someplace and invited him to come for a talk "under the rock cliff."

Lloyd came over, and he already knew there was a fight going on among the Democrats. He and I talked about it, and I suggested that the Republicans might do well to get Bill Abraham on as their candidate for sheriff.

"Goddammit, Raymond!" said Lloyd. "You know Bill Abraham's always been Democrat! He'd get in there and do whatever you wanted him to!"

"Oh, no!" I insisted. "Bill's his own man. He'd make a good sheriff—and that's all there is to it. . . . Isn't there some way you could get him on your ticket, Lloyd?"

Lloyd thought about it, and he agreed to work on it. Later, he got Bill Abraham together with some of the high-ranking Republicans in the county.

Now, the Republicans are not like the Democrats. The Democrats talk too much; everything's out in the open with them. But the Republican party doesn't talk enough. They play their cards in close and don't let anybody see what they're doing. They have just a few people making all the decisions for them. Sometimes that hurts them, but in this case it helped. It never did get out that they were planning to put Democrat Sheriff Bill Abraham on their ballot for that election. It didn't come out until the night their executive committee met.

Bill Abraham and I were sitting in the Smoke House that night, waiting for word from Lloyd. Sometime during the meeting, Lloyd poked his head into the restaurant and motioned for Bill to come over. Then Lloyd nodded to me, and I knew immediately that Bill Abraham would be chosen as the Republican nominee for sheriff.

"I'll see you later, Bill," I said, and off he went with the GOP.

Most of the Democrats laughed at that. They said there was no way that Bill Abraham could win as a Republican. But they weren't thinking. They didn't figure on our organization.

First, I had some people going over to Jack Ferrell and his crew just to keep a bug in their ear: "Jack's daddy will have *no problem* beating Bill Abraham," they said. As a result, Jack's bunch all believed that Jack's daddy would be a shoo-in for sheriff. They figured we had no power.

Meanwhile, we were out organizing for Bill Abraham. We talked to people and gathered up money to fight with. Jack had plenty of resources, but he never liked to use them. He didn't pay his people enough to get them out into the neighborhoods. He thought he had everything locked up, but he didn't have the grass roots behind him.

Election day 1966 came around, and Bill Abraham beat J. W. Ferrell, Sr., by more than a thousand votes. By God, it was just organization. We made our people work, and Jack had lost all his.

In the 1968 primary election, I was on the ballot to keep my job as county clerk. I'd done a good job as clerk, but the money was poor—just six hundred dollars a month—making it a hard job for me to keep. As the campaign went on, I got to wondering why I'd decided to run for reelection in the first place.

A man named Bill Anderson was the other faction's candidate, and they were running him hard against me. I knew I'd have to spend a whole lot of money on my campaign—a race I really didn't care to win—so I talked to a couple of my political friends and told them what I really wanted: a job at the state capitol in Charleston. They suggested we all go up there and talk the governor into working out a good job for me.

The governor at that time was Hulett C. Smith, a man I knew well. I'd supported him when he ran in 1964, and I'd also been a good friend of his daddy's.

"Raymond, you've had a lot of experience," Hulett told me when we went up there. "You ought to be able to handle a good job with state roads."

Hell, yes, I had experience! I had fourteen years of construction, a lot of it with the state road commission. I'd worked the state roads from the bottom up. I could run levels with a transom. I'd built bridges and dams. Hulett *knew* he'd do well to hire me, so he did. I became the new highways construction supervisor for West Virginia's interstate system.

With that nice a job offer, it didn't make much sense for me to be running for Logan's county clerk in the primary. At first I figured I'd just drop out, but my friends talked me out of it. They were afraid that if I dropped out someone else would come in and win the office from Bill Anderson, who was a good man and a good candidate.

So, to keep harmony in the party, I agreed to keep my name on the ballot for the primary. I just wouldn't campaign. I didn't do one damned thing for myself. I worked for our other candidates, but I never distributed any of my own literature. (A lot of it is still stored in my loft.) I made no speeches; I just stayed out of it.

But you know? Even not running, I damned near won it.

After that '68 primary, I went to Charleston to work, earning more than double what I'd made as Logan's county clerk. My job was to check on interstate construction and maintenance all over West Virginia, making sure that everything was done right.

I was still known as a good speaker then, and that really helped me in my job. I rode around in the state airplane, appearing before various groups and public hearings to tell people what the state road commission was doing in their communities. I got up there and explained the plans to everyone. I talked well because I knew what I was talking about—just like at those Cow Creek meetings. I got plenty of good write-ups in the newspapers.

My job was still political, though. Whenever I was called off somewhere, I often spoke at their Democratic political meetings. In those days, I was campaigning actively for Jim Sprouse, a progressive candidate for governor. I liked Jim. He was an independent-minded man, and he was from Mingo County, neighboring Logan. His cousin had also married one of mine.

Wherever I went—aside from speaking for the state roads and working for Jim Sprouse—I took stock of the political situation. I came back to Charleston and reported what I'd seen out in the field to Jim and his people, telling them how he was running in the state. I worked hard for Jim, but I knew he was going to lose the election, and I told him so.

The general election in 1968 was a real pity. The Democrats held all kinds of offices that year, including the governor's, but they just weren't taking care of things. Roads needed fixing and schools needed work, especially in southern West Virginia. But the Democrats weren't taking responsibility for this kind of thing, and that really hurt them politically.

Also, as I said, Jim Sprouse was his own man. He thought that he would sweep the southern part of the state, just because he was from here. But he was dead wrong. And southern West Virginia is just where he was beaten by the Republican candidate, Arch A. Moore, Jr.

Arch Moore had come from a very political family in Marshall County—up in the northern panhandle, bordering Ohio and Pennsylvania. Arch was an ambitious man. As a young fellow, he talked about holding office in Washington, and he was already a congressman by 1968. He was a shrewd politician, requiring absolute loyalty from everybody under him. All these things worked together to help Arch Moore beat Jim Sprouse that election.

The fact that I was a good speaker in the state roads department didn't cut anything with Arch Moore, and I was the first man he fired after he took office in '69. I couldn't blame him too much. My organization had worked hard against him that election, and he didn't get many votes in Logan County. Arch knew I'd been against him, so he fired me. Hell, that's politics.

At the same time, though, I really had a lot of Logan County Democrats mad at me. Jack Ferrell's bunch still controlled the County Executive Committee, and they remembered what I'd pulled with Bill Abraham two years before. And then, Bill was mad at me too. He wanted me to support him in his '68 race for reelection as sheriff, but I couldn't do that. Bill was still a Republican—I hadn't been able to get the Democrats to bring him back. If I supported Bill Abraham, I'd be forced to support the Moore administration. Supporting the Republican governor really would have soured things among the Democrats in Logan. I didn't want to split things up any worse than they already were, so I stuck tight.[1]

Arch Moore stayed in for two terms, and I didn't support him either time. All during the Moore administration, there were reports about how tightly he ran things, and about illegal deals he'd made. Those allegations, routinely carried in the *Charleston Gazette,* seemed to roll right off Arch's back. It didn't surprise me at all when the governor was indicted in 1975, but it was all just a bunch of politics to me.[2]

I was never for Arch Moore in the early days. In 1968, of course, I backed Jim Sprouse. In 1972, I'd worked for Jay Rockefeller—that's John D. Rockefeller IV.

Jay Rockefeller came into West Virginia in the early sixties as a federal youth worker. He'd been living in Washington, D.C.,

1. Bill Abraham and I have patched things up since that time. He came back to the Democrats in 1988, and I've been for him ever since. We're tough to beat when we're together.
2. Moore was accused during his second term, in December 1975, of extorting $25,000 from a banking firm that had been trying to get a charter from the state. Moore responded with a press conference, simultaneously denying the allegations and boldly announcing his candidacy for reelection. Although other members of his administration were convicted, a federal jury acquitted the governor. Moore couldn't run in 1976, though. The state's constitution bars a governor from three consecutive terms.—T. S.

before that and moved here after being named to a social-service commission by Bobby Kennedy. Within four years, Jay was involved in West Virginia politics. He won himself a seat in the state house of delegates and, in the 1968 campaign, he got elected as secretary of state.

Jay had a tough time of it, being a Democratic secretary of state under Arch Moore, who saw him as a sure rival for the governor's office. He was right. Jay ran against him in the '72 election, but Jay lost that one—partly because, as secretary of state, he'd tried to change too much too fast. Jay wanted to bring "election reform" to West Virginia, which angered some of the political bosses from the southern counties. He even tried to get some of these fellows investigated and sent away, and they didn't like that at all. A lot of them didn't work for Jay during that '72 campaign. Some turned around and supported Arch Moore, and that helped win the election for him. Jay sat out the next four years as president of West Virginia Wesleyan College, in Buckhannon.

Then, in 1976, Arch Moore couldn't run for a third term, and Jay came back to run against Republican Cecil Underwood. I had worked for Jay in '72, so I was back with him in '76, although I hadn't really talked with him much. This didn't bother me a whole lot, but when the campaign really got going I decided a meeting with Jay was something I ought to have—and something he ought to have with me.

Jay was campaigning at the Mingo County Courthouse in Williamson one afternoon, and I had driven there to see him. I was nearby when the candidate got word that his next speaking appointment in Wyoming County had canceled on him. I knew that the cancellation would leave Jay with some time on his hands, so I took advantage of the situation. He knew who I was by then, so it wasn't hard for me to get his attention. I'd had so little chance to talk with him before that, and I wanted to "sound him out" some.

"Jay, how about you and me running over to Logan?" I said. "Why don't you drive over there with me, and I'll show you some work that needs to be done."

I suggested that he ride down with me in my station wagon and have his helicopter pick him up in Logan. And that's just what happened.

We drove through Delbarton, taking the road across Cow Creek Mountain—the road I'd surveyed myself twenty years before. I told Jay how many miners and other people—all of them voters—traveled that road every day. It had taken a lot of wear in twenty years. You were never far from a pothole to steer clear of.

Jay shook his head at how bad it all looked. He was used to traveling by helicopter, so he had almost no idea of how tough it is to keep good roads on these West Virginia hills. He was amazed at the shape they were in.

"I assure you, Raymond," he said, "that when I'm elected, this road will have the money it needs to be fixed."

We came through to Barnabus and I continued the tour.

"Now we're back on U.S. 119," I said, as we got to a railroad crossing.

Jay looked at all the potholes and committed himself to repairing that road too.

I took a shortcut, and we came to an old bridge at Omar. Arch Moore had been governor for eight years, and I don't think his people ever did fix the holes in that bridge. The state road crews had just thrown pieces of sheet-iron over them. Some of the sheets had scooted loose, showing holes big enough to swallow a car wheel to its axle. Jay saw all this, and he turned to me.

"My gosh," he said, "Is this the main highway?"

"Yeah!" I said. "This is 119!"

"You mean they let things get this bad?"

"They sure do!" I said. "It's been this way for more than a year!"

"We'll have to get a new bridge there," he said, "when I'm elected."

I assured Jay Rockefeller that I'd hold him to that promise.

Jay was elected governor that year and, true to his promise, we got the Cow Creek Road widened and blacktopped all the way from Delbarton to Barnabus. Sometime after that, I called to remind him about the bridge, and he said he hadn't forgotten. Later, I saw some state engineers surveying the bridge at Rossmore.

"Hell, you've got the wrong place!" I told them. "The bridge at Omar is the one with all the holes!"

One of the engineers, a fellow who knew me, set me straight. "We've got orders to survey them all," he said.

Jay put three new bridges on Island Creek that year. Before long, the trip from Logan to Delbarton was just as smooth a ride as it could be. The whole state had a good roads program under Rockefeller. He did well enough—and spent enough money—to win himself another term in 1980. I supported him again that year but, once he was in office that second term, Jay and I got into a political clash of sorts. I wanted some things done—a road or a job for somebody. But everytime I asked for something, I seemed to get shoved off someplace. The worst thing was this: I learned that Jay and his new right-hand man, Howard Wellman, were doing business with my old rival Jack Ferrell.

I just couldn't understand it. Jack was in control of the county's Democratic Executive Committee. But he'd never done much of anything for Jay's elections. When push came to shove, I didn't think Jack ever had too much to offer them, while I'd supported Jay all along.

I took the situation as long as I could. Then I started thinking of myself as "Raymond Chafin: the dead old dodo bird." I got to thinking about it after going to bed one night. I lay there in the dark and realized I was madder than hell. It was about ten-thirty or eleven o'clock when I got up and called the governor's mansion in Charleston. A state policeman answered the phone, but he knew who I was.

"Is the governor in?"

"Yes, sir, he is."

"Wonder if I could talk to him?"

"Hold on, sir."

Jay came on. I told him I wanted to come over and meet with him.

"What about, Raymond?"

"I don't like the way some things have been going recently."

Then he said something that really set me off. "Raymond, I can't listen to two or three of you fellows over there. I've got to listen to someone, and Jack Ferrell is my friend."

"He wasn't your friend when you needed him!" I said. "But I've always been your friend, Jay! And I still want to be your friend. I don't want to have to tear up the playhouse over here. I want to get along. I need to come to Charleston and talk to you. You gonna be there in the mornin'?"

"Yes, but . . ."

"Good! I'll see you then!" And I hung up the phone.

Early the next day, I drove to Charleston and marched right into that front office—the same office where I'd gone to see all those other governors before him. A state policeman was standing there, always a dead giveaway that the boss is in.

"My name's Raymond Chafin—from Logan County," I told the receptionist. "I've got an appointment with the governor."

Now, that wasn't exactly true—Jay never actually gave me an appointment—but I was mad. They confirmed it, though. I *did* have an appointment with the governor.

Jay Rockefeller stands six foot tall and then some, which forces him to stoop a bit to welcome most other people into his office. He shook my hand, towering over me.

"Come on in, Raymond! I hope you're in a better mood this morning than you were last night!"

I walked in, and there was Howard Wellman, Jay's "junior partner" who'd been cutting me out of everything.

"Goddammit, I didn't come here to see *him*," I said. "If I thought I needed to see *this* man to get what I want, I never would have come."

But Jay wanted Howard in on the meeting, promising that he wouldn't say anything. We sat down, and Jay asked me what the matter was. I listed some promises that had been made and not kept—not just with me, but with others in Logan County. Jay wasn't getting along with several important people down there, and he was listening to the wrong ones, liable to lose the next election if things didn't change.

"I don't think so," Howard said.

"Goddammit, I didn't come over here to talk to you!" I shouted. "I'm talking to the governor. If you want to talk, I'll just leave out of here right now—and you can just keep talking to yourselves! Just try to go with whatever you *think* you've got!"

"Now, wait a minute, Raymond," Jay said, trying to calm me down. He started making some proposals. Then he turned to Howard and said, "Don't you think we can work that out?"

"I don't know," Howard answered. "I'll have to talk with Jack."

That snapped it.

"I'll tell you what you do," I said. "You can 'call Jack' and do any goddamned thing you want to. But I'm going back to Logan County, and I'm going to change the whole Executive Committee. I'm going to change the whole damned thing and, by God, I'll show you who runs that place! And I'll be damned if you won't be sorry for it! See you later, gentlemen."

I got up, and Howard said, "Well, you'll have to show me!"

"By God, I will, Junior!" I hollered. "And if I was anything like I used to be, I'd whip your ass all over this fuckin' office! But I have too much respect for *this* governor. As far as I'm concerned, you're just a low-down chickenshit!"

I looked for the policemen to come marching in to drag me out of there, but they never did. I guess the part about my respect for Jay helped.

I left Charleston, came back to Logan, and went to work. A lot of county politicians had been unhappy with the situation. Jack Ferrell had the governor's ear, and some of the coal operators were with him. But Jack just couldn't make it work for people. People wanted their roads fixed and folks in Cora had been needing a new bridge. These might not sound important, but they were vital for the upcoming '84 election. Jack Ferrell and his people hadn't done the job. After a couple of phone calls and a meeting or two, the county Democratic Executive Committee voted to change the chairmanship. Jack's man was taken out, and control was given back to me.

I could have had the chairman's seat myself, but I didn't want it. I just wanted to heat things up a little bit, to show Charleston that I could put anyone I wanted in there. We gave the chairmanship to a man named George Moore, and I think that irked Jay some. George wasn't anybody he knew, but after all his feuding with Arch, I'm sure having a man named "Moore" as Logan County's chairman was something of an irritation.

Not long afterward—in the next day or two—I got a call from the governor. I'd been watching TV with my wife.

"Well, Raymond," said Jay. "You did it, didn't you?"

"Done what? . . . Oh, yeah! That!"

"When are you coming over?"

"I don't know, Jay," I said. "How's little Junior doin'? Did I make a believer out of him?"

"You sure did."

"Are we ready to work together?"

"Sure, Raymond," he said. "We're ready to work."

"OK," I smiled. "I'll send George Moore over to see you!"

I hung up the phone and just laughed.

George and I both went up there. As we approached, Jay just looked at me and smiled. We got along pretty good after that. In the 1984 election, Jay ran for the U.S. Senate, and I supported him.

Still, I had to break with a lot of powerful state Democrats that year. They supported Clyde See for governor in the primary, but I favored Chauncey Browning, Jr., of Cow Creek. I was real disappointed that Chauncey didn't get a better shake from the state organization, including Jay. I didn't think much of Clyde See, and he said some awful things about Chauncey during that primary.

Clyde didn't do too well in Logan County. After he got the nomination, he appeared before a group at the Logan County Fieldhouse. He stood there and announced that Jack Ferrell was his man in this neck of the woods. Of course, that didn't go over too well with me, or anybody else listening that night. Everybody knew then that the smart money would be getting behind Arch Moore, who was returning as the Republican candidate that year. I supported Arch too. But even so—and despite several "promises" he'd made to us—we never did get too much from him.

13 1988: One More Time

THE COAL COMPANIES PLAY POLITICS LIKE A game of poker. They play every angle they can, and they keep their cards up close.

After Clyde See won the 1984 Democratic primary, the companies could see that they were in a tough position. If they threw all their money behind Clyde, and Arch Moore beat him, they would have been in trouble. If they'd given it all to Arch and Clyde won, they would have been in trouble. The companies were on a crack that forced them to donate both ways. So that's just what they did.

Really, company people don't give a damn who's governor, as long as it's the one who'll be the most for them when it's all over. These coal companies and big businesses are all the same. Their money people ask, "Which man is going to let me dump the most in the creek?," "Who's going to let me strip coal and scrape the trees over the hillside the way I want?," or "Who'll let me get by this law or that one?" They donate to the fellow who lets them get away with more.

My sense is that enough of these coal companies gave Arch Moore what he wanted in 1984, or he wouldn't have let them do what they did. That's what got him in trouble in federal court. It took a while, but he was charged again and convicted in 1990 of giving political favors to coal companies and getting money kicked back to himself. I think the money was so big Arch just couldn't turn it down. Now he's done some time in the penitentiary, and a few company executives got in trouble, too.[1] Playing politics that way just doesn't pay—not in the long run.

For myself, I wanted Chauncey Browning, Jr., for governor in 1984. Like his father, Chauncey had been a state attorney general; his family was from Cow Creek, and I thought he would have been the best man for the job. But the state's most powerful Democrats just couldn't get behind him in the primary. They went with Clyde See, and I couldn't go along with that. When Clyde won, I went with Arch in the general.

My support for him should have put me in a better position with Arch Moore, and, in fact, I was able to have several conversations with him. Bill Abraham was close to Arch and, sometime after the 1984 election, he got Arch to give me a call.

"Raymond, I understand you want to talk to me."

"That I do, governor," I said. "I supported you this last time around. I thought enough of you to help you win. Now I'd like us to sit down together and see if we can get some things done."

Arch set me up an appointment, and I went over to see him. From the start, I told him I didn't want anyone to know I'd been there. It was nothing crooked; some of the Logan County Republicans spent a lot time around his office—dropping off cards, giving people flowers, and so on—and I didn't want them

---

1. Arch Moore, then sixty-seven, pleaded guilty in May 1990 to charges of mail fraud, extortion, filing a false tax return, and attempting to obstruct a federal grand jury investigation. He served two years and eight months in federal prison.—T. S.

knowing I was going behind their backs to see their Republican governor. So Arch gave me a name—a phony name.

Anytime I wanted to see him I'd call Moore's office and leave a message, using this fake name. Then Arch would know to call me back. Sometimes I'd get an appointment with him—still using this name—and I'd go to see him to discuss whatever it was that we had to talk about. I went in there several times this way.

At some point, the Republican chairman in Logan County heard that Raymond Chafin had been seeing the governor, and he started complaining about it. The man told people that I wouldn't get a thing from Arch Moore unless I went through his party. That story got right back to me and just got me to thinking. As it was, I hadn't been getting much done with Arch anyway.

"Hell," I thought. "If I'm gonna have to play this game all my life, there's no use in doing anything for Arch Moore."

In 1988, Arch decided to run for reelection for his fourth term in office, and things got down to lickety split. When he started asking for my support, I put him off.

"I'll let you know," I said. I'd had more roads, some bridges and jobs—including, admittedly, one for a family member—that I wanted to get from him. I wanted to give him a chance to deliver before I threw any support behind him.

In the meantime, the Democrats picked up on the word that I'd been going in to see Arch. From what I understand, some of the bigger politicians in Charleston started thinking that they needed Raymond Chafin back. Not that I'd ever left or anything, but that's what they thought. One day in 1987, a bunch of them called me up and said they wanted to pick a governor, and they wanted my help.

It was about a year before the 1988 primary when we got together in Charleston. That meeting included about fifteen of the state's most powerful Democrats and businessmen, all of them trying to figure out who to run against Arch Moore in 1988. They wanted a campaign like we'd had for Kennedy.

They wanted me to take full charge of the thing across the southern part of the state—in Logan and Mingo and some of the other counties. I told them I wasn't able to take that kind of responsibility anymore. Still, I said I'd help them find a good candidate—and I was willing help that person win. I also told them I was willing to retake the chairmanship in Logan County and, eventually, I did exactly that.

At that meeting in Charleston, one of us would toss out a name and somebody would say, "No, you can't have him. . . . We need someone who's more independent. . . . No, that one doesn't have any money. . . . No, you can't have this one; Arch Moore has enough on him to eat him alive. . . . Arch'd wrap that one around his finger." (If you want to know the truth, some of the people we considered that day are in the federal penitentiary themselves right now!)

Sometime after this meeting, I went to visit Tod Willis, the clerk at the state senate. Lloyd Jackson, Sr., one of Lincoln County's most powerful Democrats, was there too. The three of us were just loafing around in Tod's office when Dee Caperton—a delegate from Charleston—stuck her head in the door.

"Lord have mercy," she smiled. "What are you-all doing here?"

Lloyd spoke up first.

"We're trying to pick a candidate for governor," he said.

Dee was a pretty woman and an aggressive politician. She'd been a Miss America runner-up and was real tall—"stately" is the word the newspapers always used. She knew her way around the Statehouse, so she just walked in there and started talking with us. As she stood there talking politics, and that beauty-queen smile on her face, it seemed like the most natural thing in the world for me to start building her up some.

1988: ONE MORE TIME

"You know," I said, "I think you might make a real good candidate yourself!"

Lloyd shot a nasty look at me when I said that, so I kept quiet and didn't follow it up. We talked a little more, and Dee said, "Well of all the people you've mentioned, I don't think any of them could win."

We all knew it. Finding a strong candidate against Arch Moore was a tall order. Arch was tough. He'd been accused of all kinds of things in the newspaper—from accepting kickbacks to wrongly taking money from the estate of a dead hermit—and he'd still won the governorship three times. I told Dee my thinking: We needed somebody with money, someone who looked good, and somebody who could outshine Arch Moore.

"Are you gonna be with the Democrats this time?" Dee asked me.

"One hundred percent," I said. "If we get the right candidate."

"What if I get you a good one?" she said.

"Who could you get?" asked Lloyd.

"Would you consider my husband?"

Gaston Caperton was a big insurance executive, chief of the McDonough-Caperton Insurance Group. I didn't know him at that time, but Lloyd did. He said Caperton might make a pretty good governor.

". . . But you'd never get him to run," he said, and Dee smiled at that.

"I live with him, don't I?"[2]

Lloyd asked Dee to check on it, and said we might be interested in Caperton, if he'd be willing to run.

---

2. Dee Caperton campaigned vigorously for her husband in the 1988 election. Soon after Gaston Caperton took office, the couple split and divorced. The governor has since married Rachael Worby, an accomplished orchestra conductor.—T. S.

"What do you think, Raymond?"

"I don't know him," I said, truthfully. "But if you say he's all right, he's OK with me."

A few days later, Lloyd called and asked me to meet him at an intersection along Corridor G in Lincoln County. From there, we drove to the Capertons' house in Charleston. Dee met us at the door, but she didn't stick around. I met Gaston Caperton, and he struck me as a friendly fellow, standing taller than most—which never hurts a candidate. He talked with Lloyd and me about a possible campaign.

"If you run for governor," I asked him, "Do you think you can put up a strong fight?"

Caperton told us that he could get a lot of support, but his biggest trouble would be winning the primary.

"If I get the nomination," he said, "I'm sure I can win."

I never told Caperton that I was for him; but the more we talked at that meeting, the more it seemed like this would be one hell of a good campaign.

"If I can get things lined up," he said, "I'll do it. . . . How do we start?"

We started with a poll. We hired an outfit to take a popularity poll on Gaston Caperton and, when the figures came in, they looked unbelievably bad. That poor fellow didn't have even two percent! Thirty or forty percent, on the other hand, went to Clyde See, who was coming back as a Democratic candidate in 1988.

"Lord have mercy," I said to myself. "What are we getting ourselves into here?"

Still, we decided to throw everything we had behind Caperton. I took over the chairmanship of the Logan County Democratic Executive Committee, and the Charleston group wanted me to come out and endorse Caperton publicly. This would have soured everything I never had with Arch Moore, so I discussed it with my wife and daughter.

"The man's got two percent of the vote," I said. "If we turn this thing around for him—"

"You turned it around for Kennedy," said Louise. "Couldn't you do it again?"

"I don't know."

"Maybe you're getting too old for this," she suggested. Of course, that set me off.

"The hell I am! I ain't that old! . . . Too old . . . Goddamn!"

I called up the *Charleston Gazette.*

"I'm endorsing Caperton," I told them. "I think he can win it!"

Pretty soon, the state wire services and a lot of other newspapers were calling me up. The TV stations were calling too, all of them wanting to know what was going on. The story went out all over the place that the Logan County Democratic chairman had endorsed the dark horse, Gaston Caperton—the first county chairman to do it.

Johnny Protan, the Democrats' chairman in Boone County, called me up.

"Do you really think he can win it, Raymond?"

"Hell, yeah!" I said. "Let's get behind him! Let's bring him!"

Mingo County called; same thing. "By God, let's roll!"

At some point, the phone rang and, of all people, it was Howard Wellman—Jay Rockefeller's "junior" partner who'd gotten me so riled up, back in the late seventies.

"I'd like to see you," Howard said. "I want to smoke the peace pipe with you."

Howard had gotten himself elected to the house of delegates since I stomped out on him that day. Now he was angling for a position with the Caperton campaign. I'd already told those people I didn't want a damned thing to do with him, and I figure the word had gotten back to Howard. So now he was calling me to "make peace."

"If you want to see me," I told him, "You have to come on over here to Logan."

"I'm almost afraid to do that, Raymond," he admitted. "I don't have too many friends there. I made such an ass of myself with you before. I underestimated you. . . ."

"Come on over," I said. "We'll talk."

I have to admit, it was certainly worth it for me to smoke Howard's "peace pipe." He was a powerful politician in Mercer County and some other parts of the state. He'd been Rockefeller's administrative assistant, and now he was in the house of delegates. I sure didn't want to drive him over to Clyde See, who was still running way ahead of us. I was a better politician than that.

I invited Alvis Porter, Logan County's circuit court clerk, to sit in on our meeting. Alvis had helped me get the committee chairmanship back, and I thought he'd be a good witness to whatever happened between Howard and me. The three of us met at a drive-in restaurant near Switzer, on Island Creek. We all ordered lunch, and I got right to the point.

"You've come a long way, Howard," I said. "Now let's get down to politics and let bygones be bygones. You tried to screw me one time, and I outdone you! But I'll be a gentleman with you. I'm for Caperton 100 percent, and we're gonna elect him."

"Do you actually think he can carry this county?" Howard interrupted.

By God, would this man *never* quit questioning me?

"Howard, I want to ask you one thing," I said. "Why in the goddamn-hell do you want to be for Caperton if you don't think he can win it? If I didn't think he could win, I wouldn't be *for* him!"

In the end, I convinced Howard that he'd gotten with the wrong people in the past, and he agreed to try to get along with me. I told him I didn't want him rising in the Caperton administration and "cuttin' at me" the way he had under Rockefeller.

1988: ONE MORE TIME

"By God, if you do," I said, "I'll be after your ass! . . . Now, let's work together and nominate ourselves a governor that can beat Arch Moore!"

Howard and I left that restaurant with a little more respect for each other and an agreement to cooperate better in the future.

We all went to work on it after that. I visited the other southern counties and told them what we were doing. We put on a real Kennedy-style campaign for Caperton—except without the money. We didn't have too much to work with, and a lot of the election laws had changed, but we sold people in the same way we did Kennedy in 1960.[3] We sold them on the idea that an unknown Democrat would be our best bet against Arch Moore. Clyde See was an experienced politician, but Arch had already proven he could beat Clyde, back in 1984.

I went around with Gaston Caperton, introducing him throughout the southern part of the state. We pulled people together for a lot of little meetings. We held them with old-time string bands in Man and Chapmanville, and we had some at the Logan Fieldhouse, where we gave out free hotdogs.

The women's organizations were a key factor in the 1988 Caperton campaign. Raised on politics, my daughter Margaret became a big help in pulling the women's groups together. They all came out for Caperton. He spoke well about improving schools and roads, and that went over big with them. It was also an interesting new twist on things, for me. The women were better-organized than a lot of groups I'd seen in my time, and they weren't always hunting for money like some groups in other campaigns.

---

3. West Virginia passed election reforms in 1985 that forbid candidates and their campaigners, precinct captains, leafletters, or their campaign literature to be within three hundred feet of a polling place. The laws also limit the money that can be paid to workers—including "drivers" and other "volunteers"—and better define which voters can be "assisted" at the voting booth, as well as who can "assist" them.—T.S.

In the end, it all paid off. Caperton beat Clyde See by a huge majority. Suddenly—and a little surprisingly—we found ourselves right where we wanted to be: facing the November election against Arch A. Moore, Jr.

At this point, I got to wondering about Bill Abraham, what he might do. Bill was still a Republican, and he'd even served on the state lottery commission in Arch's administration. He still had some Democratic ties, though, and he'd used them to support Caperton in the primary. This was no problem for him, politically. Arch had said he'd rather face Caperton than run against Clyde See again. But now we were getting down to the real thing, and I was wondering just where Bill Abraham stood. I went to see him, and we talked about Arch Moore. I pointed out that a lot of people seemed to be falling in line behind Caperton—the miners' union, coal operators, business people, and everybody. Finally, I told Bill that Arch Moore just couldn't win it, and asked him to sign on with us for the general.

"I don't know, Cathead," he said. (Some of my friends called me that.) "You wouldn't lead your old buddy out there just to get his head cut off, would you?"

"Have you ever known me to pick a loser?" I asked. "Caperton's gonna win!"

Bill talked it over with one of his sons, who was part owner of a coal company, and they met together with Caperton and his people. After that meeting, they took right off with it—just quit Arch and went for Gaston.

We made a real "personal" campaign out of it. We campaigned in Lincoln County, Wayne County, Boone, and Mingo. We invited all the doctors to a meeting with Caperton at one fellow's house at Mill Creek, for example. Of course, all the insurance people wanted to meet him, too—Caperton being an insurance man.

1988: ONE MORE TIME

We invited everybody, including other Democratic candidates, to come in for the big southern meetings. Some of those events drew people from eight or nine different precincts. They were a lot like those old political meetings we pulled together back in the thirties, and they really paid off for Caperton.

One of our fund-raisers was organized around a fancy railroad trip. Rick Abraham, Bill's son, had bought himself a railcar—a full-sized railroad car with a big glass observation bubble on the top. It had two rows of lounge chairs up there, seating about ten people on each side, where you could just sit and watch the scenery go by. The car had a kitchen, a dining room, and a bar. Electronic equipment piped music into every corner of it. I never saw anything like it in my life.

They tied that car onto the back of a passenger train one Sunday morning and took a big campaign ride from Charleston to the Greenbrier Hotel, in White Sulphur Springs. Caperton was on board, along with other politicians and some campaign donors. We had lunch and dinner cooked by Tank Williams, Logan's assistant schools superintendent and a former railroad chef. Tank made New York strip steaks with mushrooms, a nice tossed salad, and his own special dressing. We had drinks, poker, and just about anything you wanted on that train. I'd never ridden on a passenger train before, so I had a great time—although I would have liked the whole thing more if Caperton and Lloyd Jackson hadn't kept me busy with all their questions.

"What are we gonna do down here?" they asked. "What are we doing about this?" and "What are we gonna do about that?"

We ended up back in Charleston around eleven o'clock that night.

By this time, Arch was starting to worry about his support in the general election. He'd heard that I'd been on that train, and he called me up, saying he wanted to see me again. I agreed to come to the governor's mansion for breakfast.

I went in there at 8:00 A.M., all dressed up in my suit. Unfortunately, I'd forgotten to take off a gold campaign pin that Gaston had given me. He'd been handing out these pins to his biggest donors—people who'd given him a thousand dollars. Arch saw that button right away.

"Did you give him a thousand?" he asked.

"Hell, no!" I said. "He gave me this old thing!" I couldn't resist a joke, though, so I told Arch, "The money flows the other way with me!"

Arch knew I was never a "money man." In fact, I'd given *him* a donation in 1984. But the governor just looked at that button and shook his head.

"I'm gonna have to offset that with something," he muttered.

"Get me a diamond," I laughed, "and I'll get rid of this old piece of brass!"

We sat down to a big table, all laid out with a real country breakfast: ham, bacon, eggs, and toast. We were drinking our orange juice when Arch said, "Raymond, are you going to support me the next time around?"

"I don't know, governor," and I started to remind him that he hadn't done much of what I'd asked for in the past few years.

"Call me Arch," he said.

"Okay, Arch, I'll tell you. You're a powerful man. But you'd better be careful. I hear an awful lot of talk. I hear you're in trouble with the federals. . . ."

At that time, there were a lot of rumors flying around. It was common knowledge that U.S. attorneys were looking at the governor's 1984 campaign records. Even the newspapers were onto some of the deals that he'd been making.

"Lies-lies-lies-lies!" said Moore. "They'll never get anything on me. They've tried it before. . . ."

Before the end of the breakfast, I was telling him all the things I thought he needed to hear.

"Arch, you've got a problem," I said. "Everything that's done around here has to go through Arch Moore. You don't let anybody else handle anything. You don't have a department head anywhere who can make a decision! Before they do anything, they've got to push your button first. You're gonna be in bad shape if they ever *do* get after you, because you won't have any friends. They'll turn on you fifty different ways."

"Oh, no, I'm not that way!" he said.

"Well, that's the way I hear it."

I don't think Arch Moore liked hearing what I had to say that morning, but I didn't mind telling him. That's just the way I operate. Painting a pretty picture for a man doesn't do him any favors, and it never was any good for me. I think I rubbed Arch the wrong way because I told him the truth.

I left there, and Arch told me I could call him for anything, saying that his door was "always open." But I never did go back. Actually, Arch was already way down by that time. He didn't have the zip that he once had. My sense was that he'd turned people against him by sneaking around and not doing what he said he was going to do.

Once we got Caperton's campaign rolling, they couldn't stop us. Gaston won the support of almost every influential group in the state—all the unions, the teachers, and the companies. He ran right over top of Arch Moore, taking almost every county in West Virginia.

By the general election, I'd given up the county chairmanship in Logan. They didn't really need me after the primary and, aside from that, my wife was sick. Both she and my daughter needed me, and I decided it was time for me to spend a little more time at home.

Epilogue:
Politics Old and New

Sherwood: You're saying, then, that I'm a fool if I don't vote with a political faction.

Chafin: I'm not saying you're a fool. But you don't know anything about politics. You can vote independent if you want to, but as soon as you go to get something, well, you're not going to get it.

S**OME PEOPLE MIGHT SAY THAT RAYMOND** Chafin is getting too old to do anything today, and they may be right about some of that. But I can still speak to a crowd as good as I ever could. The bigger the crowd, the better it is with me.

I have to admit, though, a whole lot has changed today. The coal trucks go up and down Cow Creek Road, each one hauling as much as fifty tons of coal—each claiming thirty—back and forth from the strip mine where my grandparents once lived. The state and the federal people are getting after some of these operators to put the land back the way it was, and that's only right. Their companies are making plenty of money out of here. No need for them to come in and just tear us all to pieces.

There's also a big difference between the way politics is played now and the way it used to be. If you wanted to win an election, it was fist-and-skull back then. If you didn't go out

EPILOGUE: POLITICS OLD AND NEW

there and risk getting shot or killed, you didn't work an election at all. It was dangerous in those days.

But it was also more personal. My grandma and my grandpa—the Currys, the Chafins, and all their friends—stuck together. If one of them got sick, somebody always came to help. They all voted together, too, and that made them powerful. The candidates came out to where you lived. They found you in your cornfield and told you what they stood for. A man came to your house; he stopped and visited with you. They listened to you in your kitchen, and they tried to help you, to do things for you.

On election day, the faction hired people for ten or twenty-five dollars to drive a car or work the election ground. A voter might go in to choose John Jones, but we met the voters outside, talked to them, and possibly swayed them into casting a vote for Eli Hoehandle—and maybe eight or ten others on our slate. Maybe they wouldn't be for everyone you liked, but they might vote for one or two of them. That's the way the organizations worked.

The political leaders, the Democratic Executive Committee, stayed active too. We got the best people we could find to run for office—and the best ones we could find to do a job. We recommended everybody for everything, and we tried to get the best people we knew.

It seems like just about everybody votes by themselves today. That's not true in my town. Barnabus has 485 votes, and the candidates who work that precinct know they don't have to put much money at all into organizing it. They know that we're all going to be together and vote for the people we know will help us out. After the election, we can go down to the courthouse and ask for almost anything. We don't ask for things that are against the law or unethical. We ask them to take care of our roads, our bridges, and our schools. You couldn't buy ten votes on this creek today. That's not so everywhere, but that's the way it is on

Cow Creek. We vote for people we know who can get something done for us when we need it.

I'm still well known, but I don't have the power I once had. Hell, nobody does. We don't elect the same people we used to elect by voting. Today, the state limits the money you can pay drivers and election workers, and it keeps people from campaigning at the polls. But does it limit the thousands that someone can pay for television advertising? No, it doesn't. Does it restrict the things you can say on television? No, siree. Look at those TV campaigns! Not only do those commercials not tell you anything, some of them aren't fit for public consumption! If you had said such things about one of our candidates in the old days, he'd have knocked your head off.

It doesn't improve on the candidates, either. It seems like all politicians want nowadays is their own salaries. Then they want to make another dollar somewhere else. They don't do for the public like they ought to. In the old days, a sheriff who was of no account didn't stay in office. The other politicians would get rid of him. Politicians today don't want to do things the way we used to. They don't want to hold the kind of meetings we used to have. They don't want people to know what's going on. They'd rather look good on television.

The way it is now, nobody but the rich man's got a chance to win. You pay hundreds or thousands of dollars to the advertisers, and they'll say anything you want them to about the other side. A poor person running for office doesn't have any way to fight a campaign like that. There's no way they can compete.

That's what's happened to politics. That's the reason we've got these millionaires and billionaires in office today. They spend money the way that's easiest for them, and the rest of us have to fight harder to win our elections. It may not be impossible to elect the ordinary person who knows us and knows our problems, but it's a whole lot tougher.

EPILOGUE: POLITICS OLD AND NEW

For one thing, you can't sit there in your apartment and then run out there on election day to cast your vote. You don't even know who the candidates are or what they're for. You've got to learn who these people are, and you can't know that from a TV commercial. Weed out the bad ones; just get rid of them. It's not easy, and it's not the answer to all our problems, but it just might help. As for me, as long as there's an election, I want to be there.

It's probably fairly obvious by now that Raymond Chafin has no halo over his head. Well, I never claimed to be an angel. I've made some mistakes; but I've never stolen from anybody. I've done well for myself, and for the people close to me. Now I'm getting on in years, and I thought some of these stories should be told. I'm not telling them just to make myself look good. Everything you've read here is true. If it works out against me, well, no matter. Hell, that's politics!

Index

Abraham, Bill, 160–61, 162–63, 167, 184
Abraham, Rick, 185
Adams, Web, 103
Anderson, Bill, 164–65
Andrews, R. Carl, 83
Aracoma Hotel, 20, 49, 56, 57–58, 124, 127, 131, 138, 141, 143, 144, 148

Barnabus (town), 15, 16, 18–19, 26, 35, 47, 72, 73, 77, 79, 107, 114, 169, 170, 190
Barron, Wally, 140
Beaufort, Orin, 157
Berman family, 18
Bivens, Red, 112, 162
Blackballing, 42, 46, 89, 90
Black lung, 4, 154
Blair, Joe, 160
Blair Mountain war, 22–23, 50
Blue Goose (saloon), 19–20, 24
Boone County, W. Va., 149, 181, 184

Boone County Coal Company, 114
Bootlegging. *See* Moonshine
Browning, Chauncey, Sr., 95, 96, 100–02
Browning, Chauncey, Jr., 174, 176
Browning, Mary Curry, 96, 101–02
Browning, U. G., 15, 18, 43, 76, 155
Browning, Wayne, 18
Browning family, 7, 8, 95, 104
Brumfield, Lloyd, 162–63
Byrd, Robert, 105–09

Caperton, Dee, 178–79, 180
Caperton, Gaston, 179–87
Chafin, Bessie, 10, 11, 24, 25
Chafin, "Big" John, 60–74, 97–99
Chafin, Cecil, 23
Chafin, Clifton, 10
Chafin, Don, 20–24, 26, 50, 55, 60, 65, 66–69, 70, 97
Chafin, Elbert (father), 8, 29–40, 46–47
Chafin, Ester-May, 10
Chafin, Junior, 10

Chafin, Kenneth, 10
Chafin, Louise Chambers (wife), 26, 69, 72, 73, 77, 89, 114, 126, 141, 151–52, 180–81
Chafin, Lucinda Curry (mother), 8, 9–10, 19, 25, 26, 30–31, 47, 62
Chafin, Margaret (daughter), 70, 72, 126, 141, 183
Chafin, Raymond: and "Big" John Chafin, 60–74, 97–99; and 1952–59 campaigns, 94–114; and 1960 campaign, 115–50; and 1964–84 campaigns, 160–74; and 1988 campaign, 175–87; childhood of, 6–32; conclusions on politics of, 188–91; and first election (1936), 3–5, 33–43, 45–59, 63, 89–93, 151–58; and job at bowling alley, 34; on the "state roads" (1940s), 75–88; youth of, 32–45
Chafin, Thomas, 7–8
Chafin, Verna, 10
Chafin, Willie, 10
Chambers, Art, 26–27, 77
Chambers, Bill, 107
Chambers, Cynthia Raines, 26, 77
Chambers, George, 14
Chambers, Judge C. C. "Cush," 116, 117, 122, 125, 131, 137–39, 146, 147–49
Chambers, Louisa Curry, 14
Chambers, Parlee, 107
Chapmanville, 27–28, 29, 96, 97, 111, 113, 121, 137, 183
Charleston Gazette, The, 167, 181
Chauncey, W. Va., 26, 35, 61, 62, 63, 79, 80, 92
Chauncey Holler, W. Va., 27–30, 60–63, 93, 146
Chrysler Corporation, 37
Coal industry, 7, 13–14, 20, 32–33, 37, 40, 104, 188: consolidation of, 13–14; economic impact of, 153– 54, 157; and politics, 20–24, 90–96, 125, 132, 133–35, 145–46, 175–76, 184; and support for JFK, 125, 132, 133–35, 145–46. *See also* Black lung; Blair Mountain war; United Mine Workers
Combs, Grover, 94
Commodities program, 4–5, 154–56
Company store, 14. *See also* Junior Mercantile
Cook, R. J., 110
County Commission, 109–12, 114, 159–62
County Court. *See* County Commission
Cow Creek, W. Va., 4, 6–17, 19, 24, 26, 27, 29–30, 35, 43, 47, 69, 74, 76, 77–78, 79, 81, 94, 96, 111, 112, 137, 143–44, 153, 161, 174, 176, 189–90
Cow Creek Road, 12, 43–44, 77–78, 95, 100–04, 169–70
Curry, Barnabus, 6, 7, 8
Curry, Betty, 8, 9, 11
Curry, Elvie, 94, 101, 111–13, 120, 121–22, 124, 131, 137–38, 143, 145, 148
Curry, Ethel White, 76
Curry, Harley (taxi driver), 19, 20
Curry, Harley (uncle), 4, 76–78, 95, 103
Curry, Isom, 28–30
Curry, Kess, 81–83
Curry, Laura, 19
Curry, Mary Chafin, 4, 6, 14–15, 18, 27, 76, 153
Curry, Pleasant ("Plez"), 6, 10
Curry, Sally, 9
Curry, Tommy, 6, 7, 8, 10, 14, 18, 27, 76
Curry, Victor, 6, 8–9, 11, 16, 19
Curry Cemetery, 16, 74

Index

Damron, Oval, 116, 125, 131, 138, 147–48
Decoration Day, 15–17
DeFobio, Alex, 116
DeFobio family, 18–19
Democratic Executive Committee (county), 109, 110, 112, 116, 117, 121, 159, 160, 162, 167, 170, 172, 173, 180, 189
Depression, the, 31, 42, 61, 76
Dingess, Bill, 160–61, 162
Dingess, Julius, 77

Election campaigns: of 1926, 26–27; of 1936, 46–59, 63–66, 87; of 1938, 79–80; of 1944, 83–88; of 1952, 93–101, 105–08; of 1956, 109; of 1958, 109–10; of 1960, 4–5, 110–50; of 1964, 159; of 1966, 162–64; of 1968, 164–66, 167; of 1972, 167–68; of 1976, 168–70; of 1984, 173–75, 186; of 1988, 177–87
Election commissioners. *See* Election officers; Precinct captains
Election day, 46, 47–48, 56, 183: campaigning on, 46, 47–48, 56, 183; "helping" voters on, 54, 127; management of, 21, 53–55, 81, 120, 136, 144, 148–49, 188–91; violence on, 26–27, 188–89. *See also* "Lever Brothers"
Election officers, 54–55, 110, 126, 127, 134, 144. *See also* Precinct captains
Election reform, 168, 183, 190
Ellis, Claude, 116, 121–22, 132–33, 138, 141, 145, 149, 150

Feldman, Meyer, 154, 155
Ferrell, J. W., Sr., 162, 163, 164
Ferrell, Jack, 121, 159–60, 162, 163, 167, 170, 171, 172, 173, 174
Food stamp program, 155–58

Grand Ol' Opry, 41

Hager, Elizabeth, 112
Hager, Okey, 109–10, 111–12, 113–14, 116, 160
Hager, Red, 111, 112, 113–14, 116, 121
Hale, Orville, 49, 50, 55, 56–57
Harding, Warren, 23
Harkins, Arnold, 120, 122, 148
Hatfield, Carlos, 62
Hatfield, Devil Anse, 7
Hatfield, Joe, 20
Hatfield, Levicy Chafin, 7
Hatfield, Tennis, 19–20, 24, 27, 28, 29–30
Hedrick, H. H., 100
Henlawson, W. Va., 97–99
Hensley, Ed, 28–29
Holliday, O. M., 92–93
Humphrey, Hubert H., 115–16, 117, 118, 123, 125–26, 128, 130, 133, 136, 138, 139, 144, 149: and campaign spending, 115, 132, 133, 144; original support for, 115–16; popularity of, 125–26, 130, 133, 139, 144; withdrawal of from race, 149
Humphrey, Muriel, 115

Island Creek Coal Company, 25, 133–35

Jackson, Glenn, 116, 117–18, 125, 138, 147
Jackson, Lloyd, Sr., 178–80, 185
Jones, Ham, 37
Junior Mercantile (store), 33–43, 111
Justice, Nola, 113
Justice, Okey, 110–14, 116, 122, 125, 134, 137–38, 139, 147–48

Kennedy campaign, 115, 116–20, 123–24, 126–29, 132–37, 139,

141–47, 148–49: and initial Logan contacts, 116, 117; and political management, 117–18, 132–37; and spending, 115, 122, 128, 132–33, 135–37, 141–44, 149
Kennedy, Jackie, 119–20
Kennedy, John F., 4–5, 114–58, 178: and black lung, 4, 154; and Catholicism, 117–18, 123–24, 126, 147, 149; meetings with, 3–5, 117–19, 127–29, 151–56, 157; observations of West Virginia by, 128–29, 4–5, 153–54; popularity of, 123–25, 130, 147, 157–58, 137–38, 139–40, 149; and poverty issues, 4–5, 128, 153–58; as president, 4–5, 109, 151–58; visit of to Omar, 126. *See also* Kennedy campaign
Kennedy, Robert, 168
Kennedy, Rose, 141

"Lever Brothers," 127
Life (magazine), 127
Lincoln County, W. Va., 178, 180, 184
Litzen and Smith Coal Company, 61

Marland, William C., 95–96, 100–03
Martin, Dennis "Boss," 98–100
Masons, 117, 118
Massey, Morgan, 125, 145–46
McCahey, James B., Jr., 132–34, 135, 143, 146
McDonald, Ed, 140
McDonough, Robert, 142
McDowell County, W. Va., 96, 126, 134, 149, 157–58
Media, 139, 190, 191
Memorial Day. *See* Decoration Day
Mercer County, 182
Mill Creek, 63, 66, 184
Mine guards, 21–22, 66
Mingo County, W. Va., 7, 13, 22, 95, 134, 149, 166, 168, 178, 181, 184
Monroe County, W. Va., 36–38

Moonshine, 20, 22, 24, 27–30, 35, 40, 41, 43, 60, 63. *See also* Prohibition
Moore, Arch A., Jr., 166, 167, 168, 174, 175–78, 179, 183, 184, 185–87
Moore, George, 173, 174
Morrison, John, 87, 89–90
Murphy, Floyd, 94, 96–97, 98, 99, 107

Neely, M. M., 83–87
Nelson, Lonnie, 139–40
Nelson, Mitt and Bird, 28–30
Nelson, Sherman, 28, 29
New Deal. *See* Roosevelt, Franklin Delano; Works Progress Administration
Nixon, Richard M., 151

Obenshain, T. A., 35–39, 40, 41, 42
Omar, 16, 24, 25, 32, 33, 35, 38, 40, 41, 43, 60, 79, 80, 90, 103, 126, 141, 153, 169, 170
Omar Mining Company, 114, 125

Parks, Bill, 40, 42–43
Parks, Lynn, 40
Parks, Ted, 40
Patronage, 48, 53, 58–59, 63, 94–95, 123
Peddling, 12, 14–15
Perry, Chuck, 124
Perry, Ethel, 124
Perry, Lester, 121, 122, 124, 131, 138, 142–43, 145, 147, 148, 152, 162
Peterson, Esther, 155
Peytona Lumber Company, 25
Pine Creek, 18, 25, 26, 79, 81, 82
Pohe, S. C., 42
Political management, 53–55, 70, 90, 91, 112–14, 116–17, 120–21, 122–23. *See also* Election day, management of
Political meetings, 79, 96, 97, 165, 184, 191

Index

Politics. *See* Election campaign; Election day; Political management
Porter, Alvis, 160, 182
Porter, Millard, 28–30
Precinct captains, 53–55, 66, 79, 81, 82, 87, 120, 144
Prohibition, 20, 24. *See also* Moonshine
Prostitution, 70, 82
Protan, Johnny, 181

Racism, 37, 40
"Relief" program (federal). *See* Works Progress Administration
Religion, 19, 73, 123, 126. *See also* Kennedy, John F.; Catholicism
Republicans, 20, 27–28, 43, 48, 50–51, 53–55, 57, 87, 90, 145, 162–63, 166, 176; compared to Democrats, 163
Richey, Ose, 50–51, 57–59, 75
Roads. *See* State road commission
Rockefeller, John D., IV, 167–74, 181
Roosevelt, Eleanor, 119
Roosevelt, Franklin Delano, 43, 50, 51, 155

Sawyers, Burl, 102–03
Searls, Howard, 26–27
See, Clyde, 174–76, 180, 182, 183, 184
Sheriff's deputies, 21–22, 26, 66–67, 91, 97, 140
Sheriff's office, 94, 130, 159–64. *See also* Justice, Okey
Shriver, Eunice, 141
Shriver, Sargent, 132, 137
Sias, Blutcher, 84–87
Sias, Mandy, 84
Slates, 82, 123, 134, 136–37, 144, 149
Smith, Hulett C., 164–65
Smoke House restaurant, 49, 57, 127, 132, 133, 163
Sorensen, Theodore, 155

Sprouse, James, 165–66
State road commission, 48, 63–64, 75, 78, 83, 85, 164–65: and political influence, 63, 65–66, 87–88, 93, 95, 98–99, 100, 101–04, 106–07, 113, 165–66; and road taxes, 12–13
Steele, George, 45–47, 48–49, 51–53, 54–56, 57–59, 65, 75, 76, 78, 79, 80–81, 83, 84, 85, 87, 116, 144, 160
Steele, L. E., 51, 52–53, 54–56, 58–59, 75, 87
Superior Bottom, W. Va., 139–40

Tomblin, Earl, 160

Underwood, Cecil, 168
Union. *See* United Mine Workers
United Mine Workers, 21–24, 66–69, 94, 100, 134

Vote buying, 53–54, 123, 136, 150, 189. *See also* Election reform

Walnuts, black English, 38–39
Watts, Ray, 94–97, 99, 100–01, 102, 109–14, 116, 121–22, 130, 134, 138, 140, 144, 145, 149, 150
Wayne County, W. Va., 184
Wellman, Howard, 170, 172–73, 181–83
West Virginia Coal and Coke Co., 33, 35, 89, 90–94, 104
White, Ira, 70–72
White, "Mean Will," 70, 76
Williams, Tank, 185
Willis, Tod, 178
Wisconsin primary, 123
Worby, Rachael, 179
Workman, Everett, 45, 46, 47–50, 51, 56–59, 75, 83–85, 87, 88, 96
Workman, T. R., 89–91, 92, 93, 94
Works Progress Administration (WPA), 43–46, 49, 75–76, 77
Wyoming County, 134, 149